Africa
opposing viewpoints ®

OTHER BOOKS OF RELATED INTEREST

OPPOSING VIEWPOINTS SERIES

American Foreign Policy
The Breakup of the Soviet Union
Central America
Eastern Europe
Global Resources
Islam
The Middle East
The New World Order
Terrorism
The Third World
War
Weapons of Mass Destruction

CURRENT CONTROVERSIES SERIES

Europe
Hunger
Interventionism
Nationalism and Ethnic Conflict

AT ISSUE SERIES

Ethnic Conflict
The United Nations

Africa
opposing viewpoints®

William Dudley, Book Editor

David L. Bender, *Publisher*

Bruno Leone, *Executive Editor*

Bonnie Szumski, *Editorial Director*

David M. Haugen, *Managing Editor*

OPPOSING
VIEWPOINTS®
SERIES

Greenhaven Press, Inc., San Diego, California

Library of Congress Cataloging-in-Publication Data

Africa : opposing viewpoints / William Dudley, book editor.
        p.   cm. — (Opposing viewpoints series)
    Includes bibliographical references and index.
    ISBN 0-7377-0119-6 (lib. bdg. : alk. paper). —
ISBN 0-7377-0118-8 (pbk. : alk. paper)
    1. Africa—Politics and government—1960–   2. Africa—
Economic conditions—1960–   3. Human rights—Africa.
4. Wildlife management—Africa. I. Dudley, William, 1964–   .
II. Series: Opposing viewpoints series (Unnumbered)
DT30.5.A3549 2000
960.3'2—dc21   99-24848
                                                                                        CIP

Greenhaven Press, Inc., P.O. Box 289009
San Diego, CA 92198-9009

"CONGRESS SHALL MAKE NO LAW...ABRIDGING THE FREEDOM OF SPEECH, OR OF THE PRESS."

First *Amendment* to the U.S. Constitution

The basic foundation of our democracy is the First Amendment guarantee of freedom of expression. The Opposing Viewpoints Series is dedicated to the concept of this basic freedom and the idea that it is more important to practice it than to enshrine it.

CONTENTS

Chapter 3: What Is the State of Human Rights in Africa?

Chapter 4: How Should Africa's Wildlife Be Managed?

WHY CONSIDER
OPPOSING VIEWPOINTS?

"The only way in which a human being can make some
approach to knowing the whole of a subject is by hearing
what can be said about it by persons of every variety of
opinion and studying all modes in which it can be looked
at by every character of mind. No wise man ever acquired
his wisdom in any mode but this."

John Stuart Mill

In our media-intensive culture it is not difficult to find differing
opinions. Thousands of newspapers and magazines and dozens
of radio and television talk shows resound with differing points
of view. The difficulty lies in deciding which opinion to agree
with and which "experts" seem the most credible. The more in-
undated we become with differing opinions and claims, the
more essential it is to hone critical reading and thinking skills to
evaluate these ideas. Opposing Viewpoints books address this
problem directly by presenting stimulating debates that can be
used to enhance and teach these skills. The varied opinions contained in each book examine many different aspects of a single
issue. While examining these conveniently edited opposing
views, readers can develop critical thinking skills such as the
ability to compare and contrast authors' credibility, facts, argu-
mentation styles, use of persuasive techniques, and other stylis-
tic tools. In short, the Opposing Viewpoints Series is an ideal
way to attain the higher-level thinking and reading skills so essential in a culture of diverse and contradictory opinions.

In addition to providing a tool for critical thinking, Opposing
Viewpoints books challenge readers to question their own
strongly held opinions and assumptions. Most people form their
opinions on the basis of upbringing, peer pressure, and personal, cultural, or professional bias. By reading carefully bal-
anced opposing views, readers must directly confront new ideas
as well as the opinions of those with whom they disagree. This
is not to simplistically argue that everyone who reads opposing
views will—or should—change his or her opinion. Instead, the
series enhances readers' understanding of their own views by
encouraging confrontation with opposing ideas. Careful examination of others' views can lead to the readers' understanding of
the logical inconsistencies in their own opinions, perspective on

why they hold an opinion, and the consideration of the possibility that their opinion requires further evaluation.

EVALUATING OTHER OPINIONS

To ensure that this type of examination occurs, Opposing Viewpoints books present all types of opinions. Prominent spokespeople on different sides of each issue as well as well-known professionals from many disciplines challenge the reader. An additional goal of the series is to provide a forum for other, less known, or even unpopular viewpoints. The opinion of an ordinary person who has had to make the decision to cut off life support from a terminally ill relative, for example, may be just as valuable and provide just as much insight as a medical ethicist's professional opinion. The editors have two additional purposes in including these less known views. One, the editors encourage readers to respect others' opinions—even when not enhanced by professional credibility. It is only by reading or listening to and objectively evaluating others' ideas that one can determine whether they are worthy of consideration. Two, the inclusion of such viewpoints encourages the important critical thinking skill of objectively evaluating an author's credentials and bias. This evaluation will illuminate an author's reasons for taking a particular stance on an issue and will aid in readers' evaluation of the author's ideas.

As series editors of the Opposing Viewpoints Series, it is our hope that these books will give readers a deeper understanding of the issues debated and an appreciation of the complexity of even seemingly simple issues when good and honest people disagree. This awareness is particularly important in a democratic society such as ours in which people enter into public debate to determine the common good. Those with whom one disagrees should not be regarded as enemies but rather as people whose views deserve careful examination and may shed light on one's own.

Thomas Jefferson once said that "difference of opinion leads to inquiry, and inquiry to truth." Jefferson, a broadly educated man, argued that "if a nation expects to be ignorant and free . . . it expects what never was and never will be." As individuals and as a nation, it is imperative that we consider the opinions of others and examine them with skill and discernment. The Opposing Viewpoints Series is intended to help readers achieve this goal.

David L. Bender & Bruno Leone,
Series Editors

INTRODUCTION

"Disaster parades today with impunity through the length and breadth of much of Africa: war, genocide, dictatorship, military government, corruption, collapsed economy, poverty, disease, and every ill attendant upon political and social chaos."

Chinua Achebe, African writer, Another Africa, 1998.

"From South Africa to Botswana, from Ghana to Senegal, democratic governments are ushering in a new era of vitality and development."

Jesse Jackson, U.S. special envoy to Africa,
San Diego Union-Tribune, March 29, 1998.

Africa is the world's second largest continent (next to Asia) in both area and population. Its area of 11,699,000 square miles is more than three times the size of the United States, and its 1990 population of 642 million made up 12 percent of the world's total. Africa encompasses over fifty nations, ranging in size from Nigeria (with a population of more than 120 million) to small island countries such as Cape Verde (population 424,000). Africa is commonly divided into two regions delineated by the Sahara Desert, which runs through northern Africa. The countries north of the Sahara are generally considered more developed than those in sub-Saharan Africa, where most of the continent's population resides. With an estimated one thousand different languages spoken and at least as many distinct ethnic groups, Africa is perhaps the most linguistically and ethnically diverse of all the world's continents. Two hundred ethnic groups have at least half a million people; no single group accounts for more than five percent of Africa's total population.

For much of history, non-Africans have referred to Africa—especially sub-Saharan Africa—as the "Dark Continent." This was a reflection of European and American ignorance of Africa's interior geography and rich cultural and political history. Europeans established trading posts on Africa's coasts beginning in the late 1400s and over the next centuries developed an extensive trade with the peoples they encountered—a trade that included the exportation of African slaves to New World colonies. However, due to disease, topography, and African resistance, little European exploration or penetration of Africa's large interior was done until the nineteenth century. "Kept on the fringes of Africa, and ignorant of it," writes historian Robert Garfield, "Europeans turned the situation around and assumed it was Africans who were isolated. They thus created the myth of the 'Dark Continent,' though the darkness was only in European minds." Europe's rush to colonize Africa in the nineteenth century was motivated in part by a quest to "enlighten" African peoples with European religion and civilization.

In contemporary times Africa has remained a "Dark Continent" for many not because of geographic isolation or foreign ignorance, but because of the frequent humanitarian disasters and political misfortunes that have brought global attention to the region. "The next time you read about Africa in the news," writes Liberian journalist C. William Allen, "it will most likely be in a story about a military coup d'etat, political corruption, [or] a catastrophe of major proportions." Sub-Saharan Africa, which contains a tenth of the world's people, is the location of half the planet's wars and refugees and most of its famines. In the 1990s alone Africans have suffered through continuing war in Angola, a

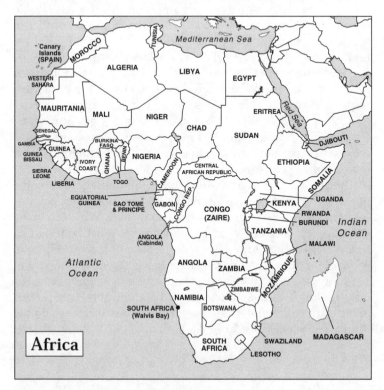

collapse of government, ethnic conflict, and starvation in Somalia, slavery and war in Sudan, genocide and massive refugee flows in Rwanda, a brutal civil war in Liberia, and political repression and corruption in many other countries. Even in nations that have escaped major wars or famines, Africans have been faced with a steady decline in their quality of life as measured by poverty rates, school enrollments, per capita incomes, and life expectancies. In his book *Out of America: A Black Man Confronts Africa*, American journalist Keith B. Richburg writes, "Africa's children are the most likely on earth to die before the age of five. Its adults are least likely to live beyond the age of fifty. Africans are, on average, more malnourished, less educated, and more likely to be infected by fatal diseases than the inhabitants of any other place."

Some observers, like Richburg, have concluded that Africa's problems of poverty, underdevelopment, conflict, and misgovernment are "intractable." Others, such as foreign policy analyst David F. Gordon and former member of Congress Howard Wolpe, have argued that such extreme pessimism is unwarranted. "While some conflict-ridden countries have deteriorated into 'failed states' featuring terrible humanitarian disasters," they assert, "other African nations are in the midst of a remarkable economic and political renewal." Wars and political conflict in some countries, such as South Africa and Mozambique, have been successfully resolved. Twenty-six African states held multiparty elections in 1996 and 1997. Infant mortality rates in Africa have declined. Economic growth rates in 21 nations were more than twice as high as respective population growth rates in 1995 and 1996. Such positive and hopeful developments, they conclude, have been obscured by "a stubborn conventional wisdom—Afro-pessimism—that views the continent as little more than a giant basket case."

The authors featured in *Africa: Opposing Viewpoints* address some of the major problems facing the continent; most offer possible solutions as well. The questions debated include: What Economic Development Strategies Are Best for Africa? What Policies Can Best Foster Peace in Africa? What Is the State of Human Rights in Africa? How Should Africa's Wildlife Be Managed? The book presents a wide range of viewpoints on countries ranging from Algeria in the north to South Africa in the south, and enables readers to gain some understanding of the issues surrounding the diverse continent of Africa.

CHAPTER 1

WHAT ECONOMIC DEVELOPMENT STRATEGIES ARE BEST FOR AFRICA?

CHAPTER PREFACE

Africa is one of the world's richest continents in natural resources, but one of the poorest in terms of human poverty. Its mineral wealth includes roughly half the world's gold, most of the world's diamonds, and large deposits of petroleum, copper, and other resources. It has tremendous potential hydroelectric power and millions of acres of untilled farmland. Yet Africa, the world's least developed continent next to Antarctica, is home to twenty-nine of the world's forty-two poorest nations. Most of its people still rely on subsistence agriculture and herding; many earn less than the equivalent of one U.S. dollar a day. In addition, African nations have built up an external debt burden of billions of dollars to foreign banks, nations, and international development agencies including the World Bank and the International Monetary Fund (IMF). "Indices of Africa's development have not only been dismal but have also lagged persistently behind other Third World regions," argues George Ayittey in his book *Africa in Chaos*.

Disagreements exist as to the cause of Africa's past poor economic record and what policies can best improve it. Some people argue that African governments are the primary problem. Many African nations after attaining independence from colonial rule embraced development strategies in which the state played a predominant economic role. African governments nationalized industries and mines, controlled trade, and created government corporations to market agricultural products and manage factories. A result, Ayittey argues, has been "the intrusion of politics into all spheres of human activity" that has stifled economic development and encouraged corruption by political leaders who viewed government "as a vehicle not to serve but to fleece the people."

In the 1980s and 1990s many African nations reversed policy, often following the "Structural Adjustment Programs" (SAPs) prescribed by the World Bank and IMF. African countries cut public worker wages, devalued currencies, and encouraged foreign investment in an effort to encourage exports and economic growth. Critics of the IMF and World Bank argue that they impose inappropriate foreign models of development on African nations. Development economist Michael Brown has criticized the international agencies for assuming that "the answer to all of Africa's problems is . . . to open up national markets to world competition and free trade," and argues that SAPs have failed to improve Africa's economic performance. The viewpoints in this chapter examine the debates over Africa's economic development and the role of outside institutions.

| "*Africa needs a faster pace of trade liberalization that would enhance the efficiency . . . of domestic producers and help it integrate more fully into the world economy.*"

AFRICA SHOULD INTEGRATE WITHIN THE GLOBAL ECONOMY

Alassane D. Ouattara

African countries must choose between two paths of economic development, argues Alassane D. Ouattara in the following viewpoint. They could continue to be hampered by stagnant economies, corrupt governments, and ethnic conflict—or they could embrace market reforms, encourage domestic and foreign private investment, and become competing players in the global economy. Ouattara outlines economic and political reforms that he believes African governments must take to achieve the latter option. Ouattara served as prime minister of Côte d'Ivoire (Ivory Coast), a nation on Africa's west coast, from 1990 to 1993. In 1994 he became deputy managing director of the International Monetary Fund (IMF), a specialized United Nations agency.

As you read, consider the following questions:

1. What economic advances have African nations made in recent years, according to Ouattara?
2. What steps does Ouattara believe African governments should take to foster free trade and economic growth?
3. What steps should African governments take to ensure the economic security of their people, according to the author?

Excerpted from Alassane D. Ouattara, "Africa: An Agenda for the Twenty-first Century," *The Brown Journal of World Affairs*, Winter/Spring 1998. Reprinted with permission.

At the dawn of the 21st century, Africa is at a crossroads. It must quickly select the path it wishes to follow. Either the continent takes its destiny squarely into its own hands, or it leaves the shaping of its future to chance or to special interests. Africa does indeed have a choice. On one hand, it can allow the forces of implosion and ethnic warfare to become the masters of its fate, to the advantage of a few potentates lacking in vision or warlords with transient alliances. Thus, history would repeat itself, with all the suffering that this entails, and this old continent will be at the mercy of all types of corruption. Africa would be stripped of the wealth of its soil and the promise of its youth and left marginalized, adrift in the wake of history.

A DIFFERENT COURSE

But Africa could just as well opt for another course. It can say "no" to marginalization and fully integrate itself into the great global village that the world has become in this Internet era. It can become one with the world so that its youth can build a future brimming with hope, grounding its action so that each and every man and woman participates in developing the nation, ensuring both transparency in the management of public affairs and a sense of a common destiny. These are the foundations of a stable, inclusive, and predictable environment. Africa has to choose between all the models of development that have been implemented in the rest of the world, including those in Asia, with all their strength and caveats.

In this viewpoint, I will first show that the economic landscape in Africa has changed dramatically in the past several years and that the seeds for a better future are germinating. Indeed, since the early 1990s, many countries in sub-Saharan Africa have been implementing sound macroeconomic policies and structural reforms to raise real per capita incomes, reduce inflation, and narrow financial imbalances. But despite these improvements, poverty remains widespread, private investment is subdued, and most African countries continue to depend heavily on external assistance. Moreover, macroeconomic imbalances are still sizable, and most countries remain highly vulnerable to changes in external conditions.

There is today a widespread consensus—both within Africa and among its international partners—that intensified efforts are required to increase growth by fostering private investment through more open markets and trade and by ensuring a more secure environment. In the second part of the viewpoint, I will review the content of such "second generation reforms," which encompass not only economic, but also political and judicial dimensions. I will conclude with the main challenges facing Africa in an increasingly globalized world.

AFRICA'S ECONOMIC RECOVERY

Sub-Saharan Africa has made substantial progress toward macroeconomic stability during the current decade. The most encouraging aspect of this turnaround is that it has been underpinned by determined efforts by an increasing number of African countries to implement sound financial policies and market-friendly structural reforms. These efforts have often been undertaken with the support of the International Monetary Fund (IMF) through its technical assistance and financial assistance under the Enhanced Structural Adjustment Facility (ESAF). This facility is specially tailored to the needs of low-income countries and is highly concessional, carrying an interest rate of 0.5 percent a year for loans which are repaid in ten equal semiannual installments, beginning 5½ years and ending ten years after the date of each disbursement. This economic "renaissance" can be illustrated with the help of a few key indicators:

• After years of stagnation, average real economic growth in sub-Saharan Africa has increased from about 1 percent in 1992 to about 5 percent in 1997 (see Table), and this positive trend is

SUB-SAHARAN AFRICA: SELECTED ECONOMIC AND FINANCIAL INDICATORS, 1990–97 (EXCLUDING NIGERIA AND SOUTH AFRICA)						
	1992	1993	1994	1995	1996	1997*
Growth rates, in percent:						
Real GDP	1	1.8	3	4.5	5.7	4.9
Real GDP, per capita	−3	−3.7	−0.7	1.7	2.3	1.8
Consumer price index	45.5	43.5	60.3	46.7	43.0	22.3
In percent of GDP:						
Gross capital formation	16.6	17.6	18.1	18.3	19.1	19.4
Domestic Savings	7.7	8.2	9.7	10.3	11.6	12.7
Central government fiscal balance	−9.2	−8.4	−7.2	−5.4	−5.2	−3.8
In percent of GDP:						
Current account balance, Including official transfers	−8.4	−8.9	−8.2	−7.5	−7.5	−6.4
External debt outstanding	98.1	108.7	135.3	123.7	117.4	106.1

*Estimated

Source: IMF, *World Economic Outlook*, October 1997.

expected to continue. The strengthening of growth has been increasingly broadly-based across countries. While in 1992 only eighteen of the forty-seven countries in the region recorded growth of 3 percent or more, by 1997 the number had increased to thirty-two. After five consecutive years of decline, real per capita Gross Domestic Product (GDP) has started to rise—some forty out of forty-seven countries are now showing a rise in their per capita incomes. This improvement has been accompanied by a welcome upturn in the ratio of gross capital formation to GDP from an average of more than 16 percent in 1992 to about 19 percent in 1997, and in domestic savings from less than 8 percent to about 13 percent over the same period. There has also been some success in bringing down inflation. Many countries have already achieved single-digit inflation rates, and for the region as a whole, average inflation (as measured by the consumer price index [CPI]) is estimated to have declined from a peak of 60 percent in 1994 to 22 percent in 1997.

• Overall, countries have also reduced their internal and external imbalances. The region's external current account deficit, including grants, has fallen from an average of about 8 percent of GDP in 1992 to an estimated 6 percent in 1997, while the overall fiscal deficit has been cut from about 9 percent of GDP to about 4 percent over the same period. Moreover, the IMF and the World Bank have recently begun implementing the framework for action to tackle the external debt burden of heavily indebted poor countries (HIPCs), including their large multilateral debt. So far, six countries, four of which are in Africa—Burkina Faso, Côte d'Ivoire, Mozambique, and Uganda—have been considered eligible under the HIPC Initiative.

• African governments have also made considerable strides in opening their economies to world trade. A good indicator of this is that thirty-one sub-Saharan African countries, almost all of them since 1992, have accepted the obligations of Article VIII of the IMF's Articles of Agreement, an agreement not to impose restrictions on payments and transfers for current transactions. Most countries have moved ahead with trade and exchange liberalization, eliminating multiple exchange rate practices and nontariff barriers, and also lowering the degree of tariff protection. Consequently, the number of countries in sub-Saharan Africa with "restrictive" regimes governing external current account transactions, i.e., goods and services, has declined substantially with the great majority (about forty) implementing "substantially liberal" trade regimes.

• Finally, the restructuring of many African economies is

gaining momentum. Throughout the continent, government intervention in economic activity is on the wane. Administrative price controls are being removed and agricultural marketing has been widely liberalized. The process of restructuring and privatizing state enterprises has been under way for some time in most countries, though with varying speed and degree of success. Labor markets are also progressively being liberalized. Fiscal reform is gaining ground: African countries are taking steps to rationalize their tax systems, to reduce exemptions, and to enhance administrative efficiency. At the same time, they are reorienting expenditures away from wasteful outlays and toward improved public investment and spending on key social services, particularly health care and primary education. On the monetary front, most countries have made progress in establishing market-determined interest rates, eliminating selective credit controls, and gradually introducing indirect instruments of monetary policy. Greater attention is also being paid to rehabilitating weak banks and promoting healthy and competitive banking sectors. In most countries, these measures, together with a lower rate of inflation, have resulted in an increase in money demand and in financial savings. However, a lot remains to be done to further improve financial intermediation and reduce the size of the non-monetized economy. . . .

CREATING A SECURE ECONOMIC ENVIRONMENT

When I took office as Prime Minister of Côte d'Ivoire, one of my first actions was to refurbish and re-equip the offices of the Supreme Court. I took this action at the time to underscore my commitment to uphold the rule of law; I refer to it today because I strongly believe in the need for widely sharing such a commitment at this juncture in Africa's economic history. Indeed, the basic objective of the "second generation" of reforms before us, to use IMF director Michel Camdessus's words, is to expand the scope for private investment by promoting greater openness in domestic and external trade and to create a more secure environment. Meanwhile, it is essential that the focus be maintained on consolidating and extending the progress made in maintaining macroeconomic stability. Let me detail this agenda before I turn to the instruments that can be used to advance it.

1) Appropriate regulations and their even-handed implementation are necessary to support free trade, which is critical for a better allocation of resources and to the spread of know-how and innovation. This requires the following actions:

Redefining the Role of Government A redefinition of the role of the government away from direct involvement in production and toward the provision of essential public services is critical. While containing total government spending within available resources, countries need to place increased emphasis on the composition of expenditure, with a view to expanding the share of outlays devoted to activities that promote growth—such as education, including that of women, health care, and basic infrastructure. There is also an increasing need to focus on the quality of the tax system and give particular attention to avoiding distortions, fostering adequate incentives to save and invest, and promoting a predictable and credible fiscal environment. At the same time, the regulatory framework should be substantially liberalized.

THE PITFALLS OF PROTECTIONISM

Protection from global competition is a dangerous nonremedy, whether it involves import barriers, high import tariffs, or currency controls. Developing countries that have been most open to trade have had the fastest growth, reducing global inequality; those least integrated into global markets, such as many African economies, have remained among the world's poorest.

Nancy Birdsall, *Foreign Policy*, Summer 1998.

More Rapid and Transparent Privatization A more rapid and transparent privatization process is needed to create a scope for the private sector. In an increasing number of sub-Saharan countries, privatization of public enterprises has become a key instrument for promoting private sector development. The experience suggests that well-defined privatization programs help governments reduce the budgetary burden of subsidies and transfers to parastatals, as well as alleviate pressures on domestic banks from nonperforming loans to public enterprises. As the operations of public enterprises are commercialized and their management and ownership privatized, the scope for private production widens, a more competitive environment emerges in domestic markets, and productivity rises. . . .

Financial Sector Reform Financial sector reform that would strengthen savings mobilization and intermediation and promote soundness of the banking system is vital. . . . In many sub-Saharan African countries, the financial sector remains weak, and hence is an obstacle to mobilizing savings, financing productive activities, and attracting and retaining private capital flows from abroad. In particular, progress in restructuring state-owned banks and strengthening the institutional environment has been slow, often because of a failure to enforce existing prudential regulations. In part, this reflects a lack of government political commitment.

Therefore, these countries will have to move decisively with structural reforms designed to deepen and broaden their financial markets; establish independent and efficient banking supervision agencies, taking advantage of available technical assistance where necessary; open their banking sectors to healthy international competition; apply best practices in bank management, particularly through privatization; address the problems of distressed banks; strengthen loan recovery; and improve the legal framework for banking activities and contract enforcement. At the same time, there is a need to develop institutions and instruments dedicated to long-term savings mobilization-stock exchanges, pension funds, insurance, and other contractual savings systems. There is also a need to explore how domestic financing facilities can be made accessible to small investors, including farmers. The sequencing of reforms— which would also have to include promoting a strong judicial system and appropriate accounting standards—is important. The IMF, in close collaboration with the World Bank and other interested parties, will continue to provide assistance in these areas through policy advice and technical assistance.

A Faster Pace of Trade Liberalization Africa needs a faster pace of trade liberalization that would enhance the efficiency and competitiveness of domestic producers and help it integrate more fully into the world economy to better exploit the opportunities of globalization. The promotion of free trade is an important element in the IMF's work and complementary to that of the World Bank and the World Trade Organization (WTO). The industrial countries could also make an important contribution to the integration of African countries into the world economy by reducing or eliminating the barriers that limit the access of African producers to their markets. . . .

ECONOMIC SECURITY FOR INDIVIDUALS

2) Ensuring economic security is critical for eliciting the participation of each and every individual in developing the nation. The steps to be taken to establish a secure economic environment are numerous:

Enhancing the Regulatory and Legal Systems The transparency, predictability, and impartiality of the regulatory and legal systems must be guaranteed. This goes well beyond the respect of private property rights and the enforcement of commercial contracts. It also involves the elimination of arbitrariness, special privileges, and ad-hoc exemptions, even where these are intended to encourage investment.

Achieving Good Governance Achieving good governance is very important. It means that national authorities spare no effort in tackling corruption and inefficiency, and in enhancing accountability. It also means reducing the scope for distortionary rent-seeking activities, eliminating wasteful or unproductive uses of public funds, and providing the necessary domestic security.

In July 1997 the Executive Board of the IMF, recognizing the importance of good governance for macroeconomic stability and sustainable growth, adopted guidelines to provide greater attention to these issues while limiting the IMF's involvement to the economic aspects of governance. The IMF's contribution focuses primarily on improving the management of public resources, in particular, through greater transparency and accountability, and supporting a liberal and stable economic and regulatory environment.

In the IMF's policy dialogue with African countries, high priority is therefore being given to the economic aspects of governance. This involves the provision of technical assistance, especially in the areas of tax reform and administration, budgetary procedures, and government financial management; improvement in these areas will reduce opportunities for bribery, corruption, and fraudulent activity. Substantial emphasis is also being given to improving the legal and judicial system to ensure respect for a fair and transparent system of property rights. In this area, the IMF draws primarily on the knowledge of other institutions, in particular, the World Bank.

Defining Property Rights Well-defined property rights are a key element of economic security for small landholders and informal entrepreneurs; they are also a key requirement for the deepening of the financial system. Meeting this need requires imagination and a close coordination with stakeholders. Simply dumping the legal instruments of advanced economies on countries with diverse cultural and administrative backgrounds will not work.

INSTRUMENTS OF DEVELOPMENT

3) A variety of instruments is available to support free trade and advance economic security. I will mention three:

Fiscal Management and Civil Service Reform A capable and efficient civil service is a key ingredient to sound public administration. However, in many countries, limited skills, overstaffing, and deteriorating remuneration in real terms have contributed to low morale, weak incentives to improve performance, and illicit activities in the civil service. For many African countries, a key step will be overhauling their civil service. After all, a lean, efficient, highly qualified, and well-paid civil service lies at the heart of good governance. The civil service reform agenda is itself a complex one; it is important that tax administration and the accounting office be strengthened at an early stage, both for equity and efficiency reasons.

The substantial progress in reducing internal and external imbalances is partly a result of fiscal consolidation. However, fiscal consolidation has come primarily from public expenditure compression. In many countries, the revenue base remains inadequate. Revenue efforts should focus on broadening the tax base and strengthening tax administration—there is little room for higher rates. It is important to articulate a comprehensive medium-term approach to tax reform that would optimize the composition of revenue and take into account the impact of tax structure on investment incentives and income distribution. Given the dependence on trade taxes, tariff reductions should be coupled with measures to minimize the risk of higher fiscal deficits. Expenditure levels will continue to be constrained by available resources, and hence the efficiency of outlays remains the key to fiscal adjustment in the short-term. As mentioned above, the composition of expenditure will need to continue to improve through the reduction of unproductive expenditures—including military expenditures—and through an increase in the share of education and health expenditure, as well as that of infrastructure.

Forging a Partnership with Civil Society Forging a partnership with civil society to build a consensus on reforms, and to provide checks and balances, is essential. To succeed, African governments need to encourage actively the participation of all the segments of civil society in economic policy debates. As evidence increasingly shows, adjustment efforts work best when reforms enjoy the broad support of the population, especially the intended beneficiaries. With this in mind, policy makers need to do a much better job of explaining the short-term costs, as well as the medium and long-term benefits, of policy options.

Regional Integration With closer economic integration, each

African country has an interest in ensuring that appropriate policies are followed in its partner countries. This could be achieved by increased coordination of national policies within a regional context. Throughout the continent, African governments are coming together to coordinate their policies, and virtually all countries are now members of regional organizations. Efficient regional cooperation allows the economies of Africa to overcome the disadvantage of their relative small size and, by providing access to larger markets, to realize economies of scale. . . . Enhancing trade links among African countries naturally also strengthens their ability to participate in trade on a global scale, and could lead toward further progress toward nondiscriminatory multilateral trade liberalization. . . .

HOPE FOR AFRICA

Economic security, good governance, and a better dialogue with civil society to build a social consensus for reforms should be the key concerns of African policy makers in the future, in addition to sound macroeconomic policies and bold structural reforms.

As I consider Africa's agenda for the 21st century, I am struck above all by its hopeful character. All items converge on the single objective of building institutions to release and support the initiative of each and every African. But I am also all too aware that African news headlines often tell a different tale, one of terrifying ethnic strife, cynical corruption, and widespread misery and disease. How can this hopeful agenda be reconciled with these stark realities? The answer lies in the power of human creativity, once it is released in a secure environment.

An African renaissance is unfolding before our eyes. Most countries, through most of their independence years, have been ruled by autocratic leaders; autocratic because, whether enlightened or not, they stood above the law. Today, the rule of law is asserting itself. It is doing so through the tenacious labors of a multitude of civil servants, of media personnel, and ordinary citizens, with the support of many local communities, and local and foreign nongovernmental organizations (NGOs). There is unfolding before us an immense and multifarious struggle between the established autocratic domination and burgeoning rules-based institutions.

More than ever before, Africans are demanding accountability and honesty from their leaders, freedom from repressive governance, and the right to participate in influencing and formulating public policy. The growing demands for more participatory systems of political representation are overdue, and will enable

African governments to build a popular consensus behind their economic and social policies. Governments can benefit from public participation in assessing the causes of existing problems, in identifying and debating alternative solutions, and in implementing appropriate strategies. Public support is more likely to be strong if there is widespread confidence that policies are applied uniformly and equitably and that there is an avoidance of hidden subsidies, for example, or special treatment of vested interest groups.

Ethnic strife and widespread misery can only be resolved under the rule of law. The fuel of ethnic strife is an autocratic system of government. It takes a rules-based system to give each and every citizen equal rights under the law, which is the foundation of peace. The same is true in the economic field: an autocratic government causes permanent exposure to whimsical and predatory taxation. Initiative, investment, and savings cannot flourish outside the security of the rule of law.

A new partnership is needed to support sustainable growth and development in Africa. International support should be—and is—focused on those African countries that have the will to break clearly with the past, and which are ready to implement far-reaching economic and political reforms. Support of corrupt governments, dictatorships, or warlords is both counterproductive and morally untenable. It is in the interest of the international community to have democracies spread and market economies develop in Africa.

Let there be no mistake: the fight for economic security is political in nature. It is a fight for the substance of power. A new basis of power exists in Africa today in all the men and women who are struggling to establish a new order. In their hopes lies my hope for a more humane Africa.

| "It is ... apparent that the ideology
of ... uncontrolled market forces,
privatisation and economic
dependence on the West has driven
Africa to this present catastrophe."

AFRICA SHOULD RESIST FOREIGN ECONOMIC EXPLOITATION

Chen Chimutengwende

Chen Chimutengwende is an environmental and health minister in Zimbabwe. He previously directed the School of Journalism at the University of Nairobi, Kenya. In the following viewpoint, he argues that African nations have become marginalized in the world economy. Following Africa's successful struggles for independence from colonial rule in the 1960s, he contends, the developed nations of Europe and the United States have since endeavored to keep African countries economically dependent on them. For Africans, the results of continued foreign exploitation have included poverty, hunger, natural resource devastation, and underdevelopment. Chimutengwende concludes that Africans must unite in a "second liberation struggle" to resist foreign domination and to promote economic development that meets basic human needs.

As you read, consider the following questions:

1. How has Africa been harmed by trade with the West, according to Chimutengwende?
2. What principles must guide the building of a new Africa, according to the author?
3. What does Chimutengwende list as the necessary tasks of organizations dedicated to the struggle for a new Africa?

Excerpted from Chen Chimutengwende, "Pan-Africanism and the Second Liberation of Africa," *Race and Class*, January–March 1997. Reprinted with permission.

It is clear that the African continent has become the sick man of the world. Africa's marginalisation in the international system has become depressingly total. It is also apparent that the ideology of unplanned and uncontrolled market forces, privatisation and economic dependence on the West has driven Africa to this present catastrophe. In order to reverse this situation, if Africa is to survive and prosper, we need what may best be called the 'second liberation' of Africa, which means its second reawakening, democratisation, unification, independence and self-reliant sustainable development.

This second liberation struggle based on Pan-Africanism has already started. It is the only process which can stop the re-colonisation of Africa. The origin and impetus of the 'second liberation for new Africa' is both local and international. Progressive internal and external forces combined are now spearheading this second liberation which will take Africa deep into the twenty-first century.

THE FIRST LIBERATION STRUGGLE

The first liberation struggle led to the independence of most African countries mainly in the 1960s and 1970s. During those two decades, the ideas of Pan-Africanism and hope gained ascendancy. The new historical period then was aimed at the achievement and consolidation of Africa's independence and development. But the most incisive and greatest Pan-Africanist of his time, President Kwame Nkrumah of Ghana, also warned of the dangers of internal and external negative forces combining their efforts to reverse or retard the process of African liberation, its gains and consolidation. He said that, in order to prevent this, Africa needed to be mass-oriented, fully committed to a human-centred development process, vigilant, united, consistently and permanently anti-neo-colonialist.

True, since the 1980s, the gains of African independence and the reality of independence itself have been seriously and visibly eroded. The achievements of Africa's first liberation struggle have been found to be difficult to consolidate in most parts of the continent. Vigilance, unity, anti-neo-colonialism, commitment and vision have been lacking. In the 1980s and 1990s, only a few African governments, like that of Zimbabwe, have managed to keep on fighting against neo-colonialism and re-colonisation, and for African unity based on collective self-reliance. Such progressive African countries are engaged in this struggle in different ways, at different levels and their pace is not the same. Forward-looking governments must be supported and encouraged to widen and intensify the fight for a new Africa.

Much has been written on what has gone wrong with post-colonial Africa. But this is a passing phase of African history. It is a period in which Africa has been trying to consolidate its independence and push for its own socio-economic advancement in the form of separate, divided and small states according to the continent's balkanisation which was carried out at the beginning of the colonial period. This balkanisation was meant to be for the benefit of western Europe and still serves this purpose. But post-colonial Africa has failed to reverse it for its own good. Without the unification of Africa, Africa will remain permanently weak and vulnerable to western machinations and exploitation. The creation of a vast African common market and the opening up of African economies to each other is a prerequisite for African development. The truth remains that we either unite or perish.

This post-colonial period, in many ways, has been a major disappointment in terms of both the pace and the results. It has been dominated by serious myths and illusions. Some essential elements have clearly been either weak or missing. The achievement of independence has often been seen as the end of history. The independence leaders, structures and state procedures have also often been treated as permanent and sacrosanct. Absolute power and the absence of democratic and practical possibilities for change caused many leaders to lose touch with reality and the people. It made them insensitive, complacent and hence blundering and dictatorial. The international dependency system has established an almost unshakeable grip on Africa. It has therefore been easy for the clock to be turned back by the retrogressive forces which are a combination of local and international elements and powers.

THE AFRICAN CONDITION

For a long time, the African population in general seems to have accepted this state of affairs. But the African condition has now deteriorated into a political and economic catastrophe. The contradictions of this phase have grown to uncontrollable proportions. The per capita growth rate in sub-Saharan Africa between 1980 and 1991 was minus 1.2 per cent. East Asia had 6.1 per cent growth rate and South Asia 3.1 per cent. Africa's per capita income is now below 1970 levels. Africa has 9 per cent of the world's population, but its contribution to the world's gross national product (GNP) is 1 per cent. Out of every three children, one goes without any primary school education. Out of every eight children, one is badly disabled. The number of malnourished children is nearly a third of the total child population. One child in every six dies before the age of five—that is, more than four million African children die every year before they reach the age of five. Africa has the highest infant mortality rate in the world, which is 108 per 1,000. The world's average is 63 per 1,000. The figure for the developed world is 12 per 1,000.

Malaria and other poverty related diseases are increasing fast in Africa. Over 50 per cent of the population has no ready access to health services, and this figure is increasing. About one third of Africa's high powered experts and professionals have left the continent for greener pastures or because of repression or non-recognition. Africa is losing more than three million hectares of fertile land every year because of desertification. Poverty leads to deforestation, land degradation and desertification. Three-quarters of all cultivatable land in Africa is now badly affected by soil erosion. Only a tenth of arable land is under cultivation. Many rural areas are overcrowded because of unfair land distribution, policies and practices. Real wages dropped to between 30 to 90 per cent of former levels. Unemployment in urban areas is now between 40 and 70 per cent.

WESTERN EXPLOITATION

The West insists on the continuous lowering of the prices of Africa's raw materials and on the regular devaluation of Africa's currencies. It always succeeds in this and it also puts tariff barriers against Africa's manufactured goods. How can Africa achieve any economic growth under such neo-colonialist exploitation? It is not surprising that sub-Saharan Africa's share of total world trade has dropped from 4 to 1 per cent. Sixty per cent of this is accounted for by South Africa and North Africa.

In order to pay for its imports and to service its debts, Africa is forced to sell more and more of its raw materials, the prices of which fall continuously, as has been said. Africa has hardly any say in the prices of its exports and imports. The volume of its exports is always increasing, while the value is always dropping. Clearly, Africa's trade relations with the West are based on naked exploitation. As a result, more than twenty sub-Saharan countries had debts in excess of their GNP in 1993. Out of the world's twenty poorest nations, sixteen are in Africa. Sub-Saharan Africa's debt is 106 per cent of gross domestic product (GDP) compared to 37.4 per cent in Latin America. Africa produces 1 per cent of the world's manufactured goods. It is also the only region in the world where it is certain that poverty will increase during the next ten years. Essentially, Africa is undergoing a period of negative development.

KEEPING AFRICA IN ITS PLACE

Within the international division of labor, the primary role of African countries has been to serve as sources of raw materials for the developed economies of the North, particularly Western Europe. As an underdeveloped sector of the capitalist world economy, Africa has been extremely useful to the developed West in this regard. Most of the relationships between these two sectors of the world economy (bilateral ties and multilateral ties through the European Union, the IMF, the World Bank, and other bodies) sought to keep Africa in its place. Thirty some years after independence, African countries remain export-oriented, raw materials producing, economies where the state has greatly expanded its role in resource extraction and in other economic activities. Depending on the natural resource endowment, countries tend to specialize in either mineral or agricultural exports. Some have relied almost exclusively on a single commodity as a foreign exchange earner: oil in Nigeria and copper in Zambia. State control of production and marketing through parastatals (state mining companies, marketing boards of agricultural products, etc.) has resulted in *privatization* of natural resources and of the state itself by a minority of wealthy citizens. In other words, state agencies and economic enterprises are managed, not for the public good, but for the private enrichment of those who control them. . . .

Africa contains some of the world's poorest people, but also some of its wealthiest individuals and families, with fortunes valued in the millions if not billions of dollars. These elites fear democracy because their predatory role in the economy requires an ability to contain popular discontent by all means necessary in order to continue extracting more resources from the people and the environment. They are class allies of the international bourgeoisie, whose support and at times military intervention were required to protect the former from their own people.

Georges Nzongola-Ntalaja, *TransAfrica Forum*, Spring 1996.

Conservative estimates put the financial outflow from Africa to the West at about US$200 million per day. For every one US dollar put into Africa, the West receives back four. These depressing statistics and facts are far from being exhausted here. Africa is actually being destroyed.

This African condition—that is, mainly mass poverty and the

ever widening gap between the rich and the poor—has become a catastrophe. The West even owns the processing plants and resources of Africa. All that Africans own are their parliaments and the power to legalise and facilitate the exploitation of their own people and their resources for the benefit of the West and a handful of well-placed Africans. This is why President Robert Mugabe of Zimbabwe strongly, consistently and rightly talks about the need to indigenise African economies and about the economic empowerment of the African people. During the last thirty years, the gap between the richest and the poorest has dramatically increased in Africa. The richest fifth now gets 150 times more income than the poorest fifth. The West, through the International Monetary Fund (IMF) and World Bank, insists that Africa should cut down expenditure on social services and welfare programmes. The ruling elites are always ready to cooperate with this because it does not affect them. They have their own cars, private schools, hospitals, etc. Cutting down on public expenditure for the poorest is the easy way out because they are almost voiceless in elections which are usually unfree and unfair. The situation is more than pathetic; it is explosive.

It is also, therefore, not difficult to find out why the economies of most African countries are in a shambles. Economic mismanagement and corruption have reached unimaginable proportions and there is a fast deepening leadership and direction crisis in most African states. Some African countries have been put in a situation where they are at a point of no return. They can only borrow more and more, yet get poorer and poorer. The state machinery is collapsing or has totally collapsed. Most of the African leaders have lost vision and no longer talk about the type of society they are striving for. They only talk about the survival of Africa as it is and its administrative politics. They are trying, hopelessly, just to manage the crisis. The number of civil wars and other political upheavals is increasing. Africa has more countries in a state of war or near war than any other region in the world. The reasons are as much internal as they are external. Such crisis and conflict can only be resolved through the second liberation and the establishment of a new Africa.

RECOLONISATION

The internal and external progressive forces are no longer in the ascendancy over African affairs. Since the 1980s, the marginalisation of Africa as a region in the global socio-economic system has developed fast and reached frightening proportions. Africa has emerged, in socio-economic terms, as the most backward, divided and foreign-dominated continent in the world, and it remains so today. In fact, Africa is now being recolonised. It is losing its sovereignty. Recolonisation is taking place through and because of the nature of Africa's relations with the West and western-controlled international agencies like the World Bank and the International Monetary Fund. Africa is moving from neo-colonialism to recolonisation—the worst form of neo-colonialism. This is being spearheaded by western multinational corporations and other large financial interests which, together, also finance and indirectly control western governments.

All this has been done in the name of freedom and democracy, and is a distortion of those concepts because, in reality, it does not mean the freedom of Africa and its peoples. Such a state of affairs is also called interdependence or globalisation which, in this case, are mere euphemisms for the dependency, westernisation, dehumanisation and recolonisation of Africa and its peoples, both in Africa and in the diaspora. The West insists on democracy, human rights and free competition only at the national level because it knows that its supporters and companies will get an unfair advantage. The West's definition of human rights excludes economic rights. During colonialism, western governments were opposed to human rights in the colonies. But now they insist on them. Yet, at the international level, they unequivocally oppose democracy. Their attitude to the United Nations (UN) is a good example of this. They strongly oppose the democratisation of the international relations system and the UN.

The factors and conditions which brought about the two world systems and the East-West conflict or the cold war still exist. What prevails in the world today is a temporary defeat of the progressive forces, which has resulted in a temporary, false global unity and consensus. The old international division of labour, based on western imperialism, is now being crudely intensified. This also automatically brings back the old struggle and language of left versus right, progressives versus reactionaries. But this false global consensus is now being and must be exposed for what it is.

INJUSTICE BRINGS RESISTANCE

As history teaches us, whenever there is injustice or oppression, there will be, sooner or later, a resistance. This resistance starts small and weak but inevitably grows, becoming, in the end, unconquerable. As the saying goes: a long journey has to start with a single step. As far as Africa is concerned, its internal and external progressive forces have already started regrouping, networking and strategising for the second phase of the liberation process. This regrouping and networking must surely grow into a victorious movement like the first liberation struggle. What motivated the people of Africa to rise up against colonialism will motivate them to fight against neo-colonialism and recolonisation. This fight will be fully backed, as in the past, by people of African descent internationally and progressive forces worldwide.

This second phase, or second liberation struggle of Africa, is emerging with better vision, more experience and deeper determination than ever before. The aim is a new Africa which will collectively, and as a whole, engage ruthlessly and effectively and systematically in a movement for the speedy reduction, and eventual elimination of mass poverty, squalor, endemic diseases, illiteracy, unemployment, injustice, corruption, ethnic wars, rural neglect—all the underdevelopment problems which characterise most post-colonial societies, especially in the African continent.

A NEW AFRICA

The new Africa that is envisaged here is to be based on the principles of Pan-Africanism; Afro-Arab unity; South-South cooperation and solidarity; progressive internationalism; socio-economic democracy; open debate on all public issues; mass participation in development projects and decision-making processes. It is to be based on people-oriented and environmentally sustainable development; self-reliance; economic and social human rights; women's rights; freedom of the press and association; probity and accountability; transparency; pluralism in matters of politics and religion; a permanent liberation process, and checks and balances in the socio-economic system. Solidarity with the poor, oppressed, discriminated against and disadvantaged peoples internationally will be unwavering. The satisfaction of basic human needs will become the number one priority in such a new Africa. Production and development will be based mainly on domestic demand. Indigenous designed growth models will, for a change, be given a chance.

In a new Africa, the movement against corruption, nepotism, regionalism, ethnic chauvinism and the foreign domination of African cultures and values, together with the struggle for socio-economic democracy and human-centred development, will be recognised and promoted by the state and the people as a permanent process. New Africa will, at both local and continental levels, have a permanent and effective mechanism for conflict prevention, control and resolution. As a genuinely independent entity, new Africa will, by its very nature, have the capability to make a decisive contribution to world peace and to the restructuring and democratisation of the international relations system.

More and more organisations or structures to serve as instruments, voices and channels of research, mass communication work and action for a new Africa are needed, both locally and internationally, so that they can support each other. And their collective effort can make an ever-growing impact in pushing forward the struggle for a new Africa. . . .

TASKS OF THE PAN-AFRICA MOVEMENT
The tasks for such organisations should be, among others:

- To defend and to champion Africa's vision, aspirations, rights, image, the cause of Africa's second liberation, and to expose the myth of the invincibility of the ideology of uncontrolled market forces and privatisation.
- To counteract any misrepresentation of facts on Africa and the whole question of Africa's second liberation in the international mass communications media.
- To promote the democratisation of society and international relations as a permanent process, continuously exposing iniquitous relations between Africa and the other regions and powers of the world.
- To defend and champion the rights and obligations of media practitioners, writers and intellectuals as communicators for, and as agents of, Pan-Africanist change and development.
- To establish and/or support programmes for the mass education and mobilisation of the African people, the African diaspora, revolutionary internationalists and any other friends of Africa internationally in support of the creation and development of a self-reliant Africa.
- To conduct research and carry out lobbying on internal and international conflict issues affecting African countries, with the aim of fostering an understanding of the conditions for peaceful resolution of such conflicts and for just and durable peace.
- To resuscitate and maintain strong linkages and support lines, and to facilitate the continuous redefinition of common objectives among Pan-Africanists and revolutionary internationalists all over the world for a new Africa.

The organisations that carry out such tasks need to coordinate their activities closely as a way of building a powerful and effective global Pan-African movement. Such organisations and groups should be affiliated to or in contact with the Secretariat of the Pan-African Movement which is based in Kampala, Uganda, and was responsible for organising the seventh Pan-African Congress held in Kampala in April 1994. This was attended by Pan-Africanists from all over the world. It must be noted that the freedom and dignity of the African diaspora and of black people internationally are permanently linked up with that of the African continent itself.

MASS COMMUNICATION

In the development of any such struggle or process as the second liberation of Africa, the mass dissemination of agitational information and the spread of ideas at both popular and scientific levels are crucial. Research, publishing and general mass communication work have an essential role to play in the conscientisation and mobilisation of the people. New Africa support organisations and activists need to realise that mass communications media can be very effective in raising consciousness and aspirations; focusing attention; widening mental horizons; giving legitimacy to values and institutions; conferring status and validity. They can encourage informed debate, help to set the national and international agendas, expose injustice, unfairness and corruption; attack retrogressive forces and tendencies, and counteract the enemy's propaganda and misinformation. New Africa support organisations and activists will, therefore, need to be fully engaged in mass communication work utilising the relevant media techniques and strategies at both the local and the international levels in the struggle for a new Africa.

| "Economic security and good governance, coupled with sound macroeconomic policies and structural reforms, should be the motto for Africa in the twenty-first century."

AFRICA SHOULD EMBRACE THE PRESCRIPTIONS OF THE WORLD BANK AND IMF

Evangelos A. Calamitsis

The International Monetary Fund (IMF) and the World Bank are both specialized agencies of the United Nations. Both institutions have been heavily involved in Africa. In the 1970s and 1980s they instituted "Structural Adjustment Programs" (SAPs) in which they lent money to African nations with attached conditions designed to promote exports and stimulate economic growth. These mandates included currency devaluations, government spending reductions, trade rule liberalization, and the promotion of private savings and investment. In the following viewpoint, Evangelos A. Calamitsis, director of the IMF's African department, defends SAPs and other IMF and World Bank programs and policy prescriptions. African countries must continue to reform their governments and economic policies to protect private property rights and monetary stability, he argues.

As you read, consider the following questions:

1. What evidence does Calamitsis cite to support his argument that Africa is in a state of economic recovery?
2. What two main concerns are essential to maintain Africa's economic progress, according to the author?

Excerpted from Evangelos A. Calamitsis, "Africa's Recent Economic Performance and Challenges and the Role of the IMF," a speech given at the Seminar of the Foundation for Advanced Studies in International Development, Tokyo, Japan, July 10, 1998. Reprinted by permission of the International Monetary Fund.

In many respects, the Africa of today is quite different from that of the 1980s. For the first time in a generation, there is encouraging economic progress in many countries, reflecting the implementation of sound economic policies, coupled with a steady movement toward rules-based institutions and participatory forms of government that foster consensus between the state and civil society.

But it is also clear that Africa still has a long way to go to make up for the ground lost during the 1980s. Economic growth rates are still not high enough to make a real dent in the pervasive poverty. Investment remains subdued, limiting the efforts to diversify economic structures and accelerate growth. Furthermore, a number of countries have only recently emerged from civil wars that have severely set back their development efforts, while new flames of conflict have sadly erupted in other parts of the continent.

Africa therefore faces major challenges: to raise growth and to reduce poverty; to build up its human resources; and to create an environment that encourages the development of the private sector. At the same time, globalization has raised the stakes for all countries, especially those in Africa, offering greater opportunities for faster economic growth but also significantly raising the risk of marginalization for those that fail to integrate into the global economy. Moreover, the [1997–98 economic] crisis in Asia has made it clear that it is not enough merely to open up economies. Sound and fully transparent macroeconomic policies, solid and well-supervised financial systems, and good governance are also essential in order to avoid serious problems and to benefit fully and durably from access to globalized markets.

AN ENCOURAGING ECONOMIC RECOVERY

Recent economic performance in most of Africa has been encouraging. After almost two decades of stagnation and decline, real gross domestic product (GDP) in sub-Saharan Africa is now growing at an average rate of 4–5 percent a year, and real per capita incomes are rising in about 40 countries. Average inflation came down from a peak of some 45 percent in 1994 to an estimated 13 percent in 1997, and only 15 sub-Saharan African countries still had double-digit inflation rates in 1997, compared with 35 in 1994. Internal and external financial imbalances have also been reduced. The average overall fiscal deficit (before grants) was halved between 1992 and 1997, to about 4½ percent of GDP, while the average external current account deficit (again before grants) fell from 5½ percent of GDP to 4 percent over the same period. These improvements have been accompanied by a slight upturn in investment ratios.

SUB-SAHARAN AFRICA: SELECTED ECONOMIC AND FINANCIAL INDICATORS, 1992–98[1]

	1992	1993	1994	1995	1996	1997 Est.	1998 Proj.
	(Changes in percent)						
Real GDP	0.1	1.5	2.2	4.1	4.9	4.0	4.2
Real GDP per capita	−3.9	−2.4	−0.6	1.7	1.6	0.8	1.1
Consumer prices (average)	37.7	39.1	44.4	40.5	32.8	13.2	9.1
	(In percent of GDP)						
Domestic investment	16.6	16.1	17.6	17.9	17.7	17.1	18.3
Domestic saving	14.7	13.7	15.5	15.5	16.8	15.9	15.5
Central government fiscal balance[2]	−9.1	−8.6	−7.8	−6.1	−5.8	−4.6	−4.4
External current account balance[2]	−5.5	−6.0	−5.7	−6.1	−3.3	−4.0	−6.0
External public debt outstanding	55.5	62.5	70.4	65.7	64.1	60.3	59.6

[1]Including Nigeria and South Africa.
[2]Excluding official transfers.

Source: IMF, African Department.

Unlike other "recoveries" in the past, the present upturn has been largely homegrown. It reflects the good policies that an increasing number of sub-Saharan African countries have been implementing for several years, often in the context of structural adjustment programs supported by the International Monetary Fund (IMF) and the World Bank. And because it has been homegrown, it is more likely to endure. Prudent financial policies have reduced domestic and external imbalances. At the same time, important structural reforms, including the removal of domestic price controls, the liberalization of exchange and trade systems, the restructuring or privatization of public enterprises, and reforms of labor legislation and investment codes, have contributed to eliminating distortions and strengthening overall economic efficiency. Many countries have also carried out substantial reforms of their agricultural marketing systems, often allowing higher prices to be paid to producers and thus directly raising rural incomes.

Increasing attention has also been paid to achieving what the Managing Director of the IMF has called high-quality growth—with lasting employment gains and poverty reduction, greater equality of income through greater equality of opportunity, and environmental protection. Indeed, Fund-supported programs have emphasized increasingly the protection of public spending on health care, education, and other basic social services. Thus, on average, countries implementing such programs have raised their spending on health and education both in terms of total government expenditure and of GDP during the program periods, and many have achieved noticeable improvements in their health and education indicators.

THE NEED FOR HIGHER GROWTH

Although recent trends have been encouraging, there are several reasons why the improvements of the last few years are not enough, and why more needs to be done to accelerate economic growth. In my view, two key considerations need to be borne in mind:

• *Growth must increase in order to achieve a lasting reduction in poverty.*

As Africa's population has been growing at about 2.8 percent a year over the last decade, real GDP should rise at least twice as fast to achieve a significant reduction in poverty and to catch up with other developing countries. Looked at from another perspective, much faster growth is required to absorb the rapidly rising labor force and materially improve living conditions. There is thus a need to raise average real GDP growth rates to some 7–8 percent a year on a sustainable basis. These rates may seem high compared to past performance in Africa, but several countries in the continent (such as Côte d'Ivoire, Mozambique, and Uganda) have already demonstrated that they are not out of reach.

• *Saving and investment must increase.*

Other things being equal, attaining such high growth rates over long periods of time would imply investment-to-GDP ratios in excess of 25 percent, similar to those achieved in the periods of sustained high growth in Asian countries. Although investment ratios in Africa have risen to 17–18 percent of GDP in recent years, these levels are clearly too low. This means that, compared to other developing regions, Africa is absorbing less of the more-advanced technology embodied in new capital goods, and its productive efficiency is consequently lower than it could be. Given its low saving and its small share of capital flows into the developing world, Africa remains heavily dependent on official development assistance for financing investment. But this assistance has been on a downward trend in recent years. Africa will therefore have to achieve substantially higher rates of domestic saving and attract foreign direct investment in order to accelerate its growth and development.

41

POLICIES FOR MORE DYNAMIC GROWTH

Private investment requires a conducive environment, one that provides confidence in the predictability and appropriateness of macroeconomic policies; the availability of the necessary core infrastructure and qualified labor; an evenhanded, efficient, and transparent regulatory framework; and a clear government commitment to foster private sector development. The reform efforts under way in most African countries have represented important steps in the right direction, but they need to be accelerated and extended to add credibility to the commitment of the authorities, particularly to the rule of law and good governance. Such an acceleration will signal to the private sector, both at home and abroad, that African governments are indeed seeking to address *all* the structural shortcomings of their economies and create the conditions for productive private economic activity.

AFRICA'S PROGRESS

After two decades of lost opportunities, Africa's economic performance has improved and the outlook has brightened. Together with [Zimbabwe] President [Robert] Mugabe we can speak of a "Renaissance of Africa." Real GDP for the region as a whole is growing at an annual rate of 4–5 percent, and per capita incomes are on the rise. African countries—especially those pursuing programs supported by the IMF, the World Bank and the African Development Bank—are increasingly partaking in the economic recovery. In the early 1990s, fewer than 20 enjoyed growth rates of 3 percent or more. But by 1997, the number of countries had doubled to about 40. Inflation has also come down sharply—with the average rate falling from a peak of close to 36 percent in 1994 to about 10 percent in 1997. Fiscal deficits have been cut by half in the past five years and external current account deficits, after widening slightly in the mid-1990s, were down to 2.5 percent of GDP in 1997. All this constitutes a remarkable reversal of the trend: from a constant drift toward poverty toward continuous positive per capita growth rates.

Michel Camdessus, address before the Organization of African Unity, June 9, 1998.

As we reflect upon Africa's economic reform agenda for the period ahead, let me highlight two overarching concerns. First, I believe it is critically important to establish and nurture an environment of *economic security* that would foster private saving and investment and, hence, promote more dynamic and sustainable growth. In many, if not most, African countries, the *legal and regulatory framework* is still fraught with weaknesses and uncertainties that hamper investor decision making. And the *judicial system*, after many years of neglect and political interference, is often ill-equipped to administer justice fairly and impartially. Private property rights are not adequately protected, and commercial contracts are not well enforced. Thus, quite apart from the specific aspects of Africa's economic policies, a key element of the reform agenda must be a far-reaching reform of the legal and regulatory framework and its administration, with a view to creating economic security and strengthening confidence. Second, *good governance* in all of its aspects needs to be forcefully promoted. In particular, every effort should be made to eliminate unproductive government spending, and to ensure full transparency and accountability in the management of public resources. Government operations must be conducted in an irreproachable manner, and all forms of corruption, nepotism, and cronyism should be shunned.

Apart from these overarching concerns, which should be at the heart of Africa's reform agenda, there are, of course, many other areas where parallel actions will have to be pursued. I am sure you will not be surprised when I say that most African countries still need to fully *restore and consolidate macroeconomic stability* by continuing to implement prudent fiscal and monetary policies. In particular, fiscal consolidation and an increase in public saving will be essential, requiring, inter alia, a strengthening of tax and customs administration. African countries also need to *strengthen their human resource base and institutional capacity* through improvements in basic health care, primary education, and vocational training, as well as to *rehabilitate and extend key economic infrastructure.* Finally, they need to *accelerate and deepen structural reforms* in several areas. Apart from economic security and good governance, I would stress five areas where a more determined pace of policy implementation is critical to Africa's future growth and development:

- *More rapid trade liberalization.* . . .
- *Financial sector reform.* . . .
- *Public enterprise restructuring and privatization.* . . .
- *Civil service reform and capacity building.* . . .
- *Regional integration.* . . .

Economic security and good governance, coupled with sound macroeconomic policies and structural reforms, should be the motto for Africa in the twenty-first century. As a number of African countries have shown in recent years, this recipe for higher, sustainable growth is certainly within the capacity of most countries. . . .

THE ROLE OF THE IMF

Africa's success will depend largely on its own homegrown efforts. But Africa's international partners, including the IMF, will also have an important role to play. Industrial countries can contribute to Africa's success by pursuing economic policies that promote world economic growth and stability; opening their markets to products in which African countries have, or can develop, a comparative advantage, and phasing out distortionary protective practices; strengthening their bilateral assistance to countries committed to strong reform programs, particularly where such programs might entail additional transitional costs; cooperating actively in the fight against corruption in all its forms; and ensuring that the multilateral institutions have the necessary resources to support adjustment and reform programs.

The international financial institutions, for their part, will also have to continue to support Africa's adjustment and reform efforts through appropriate policy advice, and financial and technical assistance, as well as training. As you know, the IMF has been very active in all of these areas, in close collaboration with the World Bank, the African Development Bank, and Africa's major bilateral partners. In this regard, you may ask, how does the IMF see its role in Africa in the future?

• First, the IMF is taking steps to put the Enhanced Structural Adjustment Facility, or ESAF—our concessional loan facility with an interest rate of 0.5 percent—on a permanent footing by securing the necessary resources to make it self-sustaining by the year 2005. Today, 23 sub-Saharan African countries are implementing ESAF-supported programs, with financial commitments totaling some US$3.5 billion. We are also taking steps to enhance the efficiency of the ESAF. Drawing on the recent internal and external evaluations of the implementation of ESAF-supported programs, we will be fostering national ownership of such programs, as well as strengthening our collaboration with the World Bank in order to improve the quality of our joint assistance to ESAF countries. In this context, we will be refocusing our efforts to help accelerate public enterprise and financial sector reforms; identify and address more fully the potential adverse social consequences of reforms; and assess the countries' medium-term investment needs and their capacity to attract and absorb external financing.

• Second, together with the World Bank, we have been moving rapidly to implement the debt Initiative for the Heavily In-debted Poor Countries (the HIPC Initiative), the majority of which are in Africa. In the 18 months since the launching of the HIPC Initiative in 1996, six countries, including four in Africa (Burkina Faso, Côte d'Ivoire, Mozambique, and Uganda) have received commitments of assistance from all creditors totaling about US$6 billion in nominal terms; in the case of Uganda, which has reached its completion point under the Initiative, the Fund's contribution has already been disbursed. Of course, to qualify for assistance under the HIPC Initiative, eligible coun-tries need to establish a strong track record of adjustment. I am hopeful that many more countries will do so in the period ahead, and that the list of beneficiaries will be much longer by the year 2000.

• Third, since 1995, the IMF has had a special policy to pro-vide emergency post-conflict assistance to countries that have undergone political turmoil, civil unrest, or international armed conflict. Rwanda is the first African country to benefit from this new policy. The Republic of Congo is the next in line, and we are having discussions with other countries as well.

• Fourth, the Fund will continue to provide and intensify its training and technical assistance for capacity building and insti-tutional reform, working both directly with African govern-ments themselves and in close collaboration with other donors. Accordingly, we are expanding the training activities of the IMF Institute and intend to establish a regional training institute in Africa, jointly with other partners in the region. We are also strengthening our technical assistance programs in banking, public finance, and statistics.

• Fifth, in recognition of the importance of good governance for macroeconomic stability and sustainable growth, the Fund's Executive Board issued guidelines in July 1997 regarding gover-nance issues that call for a more proactive approach in advocat-ing policies and helping our member countries to eliminate op-portunities for bribery, corruption, and fraudulent activity in the management of public resources. This approach includes en-couraging Fund members to improve the accuracy, timeliness, and comprehensiveness of economic information by meeting new data dissemination standards, as well as to observe interna-tional best practices in fiscal transparency (based on a "fiscal code of conduct").

• Finally, . . . the Fund is examining ways to reform the archi-tecture of the international financial system so as to limit the oc-currence and intensity of future shocks to the system. Greater stability in world economic conditions will facilitate Africa's efforts to compete in world markets and to attract international capital flows.

A FULL AGENDA

As you can see, Africa's reform agenda is full. However, if rigorously implemented, with the support of Africa's international partners, it should help produce the desired results of higher, sustainable growth and a durable reduction in poverty. And as economic and social progress takes hold throughout the continent, confidence in Africa's future will increase, and the image of Africa itself will gradually change for the better. We thus all need to work together to sustain Africa's progress.

| "The end result of structural adjustment programs . . . can be a country that is . . . more impoverished."

AFRICA SHOULD REJECT THE PRESCRIPTIONS OF THE WORLD BANK AND IMF

Dennis Brutus

Dennis Brutus argues in the following viewpoint that Africa is being harmed by economic policies dictated by the "Structural Adjustment Programs" of the World Bank and the International Monetary Fund (IMF). These international financial institutions are following the agenda of developed countries who seek to re-colonize Africa, he contends. They are forcing African nations to harm the welfare of their own people by devaluing their currencies and slashing funding for government programs and education. Brutus, a writer and professor in the University of Pittsburgh's African studies department, is a former resident of South Africa who was imprisoned and later exiled from that country for his political activism.

As you read, consider the following questions:

1. What vision of the world order has emerged since the end of the cold war, according to Brutus?
2. What are the inevitable results for countries that implement World Bank "Structural Adjustment Programs," according to the author?
3. What alternatives does Brutus believe exist for Africa's economic development?

Excerpted from Dennis Brutus, "Africa 2000 in the New Global Context: A Commentary," *Africa Today*, October 21, 1997. Reprinted by permission of *Africa Today*. Endnotes in the original have been omitted in this reprint.

As we prepare to enter the third millennium, a new political and economic agenda is being designed for Africa that will deeply affect the lives of its people far beyond the year 2000. What are the contents of this agenda, its implications, and some of the possibilities it opens?

A New Global Vision

Since the end of the Cold War, a new global vision has emerged with the shift to a unipolar world dominated by only one super-power. The presumed demise of the conflict between capitalism and socialism has so changed the global political landscape that Francis Fukuyama [foreign policy analyst and author of *The End of History and the Last Man*] has even suggested that we are witnessing "the end of history." According to Fukuyama, we are moving toward a world where major political and economic trends and patterns can be expected to remain essentially unchanged. I believe such a vision is a world where power will always be in the hands of those who now possess it, and the powerless will (unfortunately) continue to remain so—a world where the rich will get richer and the poor will get poorer. Politicians as well as academics are spreading this new orthodoxy.

This trend is upheld by the World Bank and the International Monetary Fund (IMF) according to guidelines that were established in 1944 at the Bretton Woods conference in New Hampshire, where policies were devised to prevent the type of political and economic disruptions brought about by World War II. These two institutions recently celebrated their fiftieth anniversary. Perhaps what they were also celebrating is their capability to impose the agenda that issued from Bretton Woods, which they were unable to realize during the Cold War due to the existence of a conflictual world dominated by two nuclear superpowers.

Glimpses of this agenda, particularly as it affects Africa and other "less-developed" regions, can be caught from a statement made in 1992 by Lawrence Summers, who was then chief economist of the World Bank and is now deputy secretary of the treasury in the Clinton administration. In an internal memo leaked to the press, Summers proposed that the toxic waste of the "first world" be shipped to the countries of the "third world." He argued that the Third World has more space for such waste and that the cost of treating the diseases produced by nuclear waste is much lower in these countries. Summers's views are typical of those who are shaping World Bank policies.

The World Bank asserts that the causes of Africa's economic bankruptcy are the corruption and inefficiency of its political class and its wasteful government spending, including that for education. What Africa needs, according to the World Bank, is not more educated people—professionals, people with managerial skills—but rather more people who have "practical" skills, whether in agriculture or industry. "Capacity," not education, is the key word in this context, and the World Bank has appointed itself as the agency to provide it, as we learn from their 1991 document "Africa Capacity Building Initiative."

What the World Bank has recommended are both massive cuts in the education budgets of African countries—spending cuts reaching 50 percent for some universities (for buildings and salaries of staff and teachers)—and cuts in enrollment. Paul Johnson, a writer for the *New York Times Magazine*, describes such external initiatives in an April 18, 1993, article entitled "Colonialism's Back and Not a Moment Too Soon." In this article, Johnson makes three points about African countries: (1) they are economically bankrupt; (2) they have discovered that they cannot govern themselves; and (3) they are now asking the colonial powers to return to run them. As unbelievable as these assertions may seem, they reflect the position of both the World Bank and the IMF as they extend their hegemony over Africa and other "less-developed" regions of the planet.

TRAGEDY IN MOZAMBIQUE

Most members of Mozambique's government don't find it easy to answer questions about what's happening to their country two years after remarkably successful multi-party elections in 1994. The problem is that the trumpet they have to blow—about economic growth and stabilizing inflation—isn't their own. It's got a very prominent 'Made in Washington DC' stamp on it.

According to one of the country's leading economists, Carlos Castel-Branco, the tragedy of present-day Mozambique is that a freely elected government—in which so much hope had been invested—has been reduced to a headless chicken, rushing around madly, meeting one IMF or World Bank condition after another, with no time to develop an economic strategy of its own.

Mark Whitaker, *New Internationalist*, January/February 1997.

One of the central mechanisms by which this recolonization process is carried out is the loan system through structural adjustment programs. Significantly, many of the countries that received loans from the World Bank have not seen their economies improve. Quite the opposite. Some are in a far worse economic position and more indebted than they were prior to taking the loans.

Once a loan is taken, paying it back can be a back-breaking matter. But this is only a part of the problem. Even more pernicious is that the World Bank often dictates how the borrowed money is to be spent, which is specified through a whole set of "conditionalities." One of them is the drastic reduction in public spending for higher education, which can be cut by as much as 50 percent. Other conditions include equally devastating cuts in the number of civil servants and massive currency devaluations that dramatically diminish the purchasing power of many Africans, while at the same time dramatically increasing the cost of imported products.

In the case of South Africa, which is still negotiating with the World Bank, such structural adjustment policies are referred to as a "rationalization" program. The implication is that there is something quite irrational—that needs to be corrected—about the number of university instructors and students who are in professional programs. While the debate continues in South Africa, some of the World Bank's conditionalities are already being carried out, including the sale of South African Airways. The World Bank is also insisting that South Africa remove any minimum wage legislation. The existence of a minimum wage is seen as a major flaw. In addition, the South African government, under Nelson Mandela, has been asked to promise that it will not allow workers to strike.

The end result of structural adjustment programs, such as those proposed for South Africa, can be a country that is even more bankrupt, more unable to repay its loans, and more impoverished, as its currency is devalued, its services are gutted, and its agricultural sector is turned upside down to produce cash crops for export rather than food for the people's subsistence. This has been the case in Zimbabwe, where the World Bank persuaded the government to shift production supports from food crops like maize to export crops like tobacco. Not surprisingly, malnutrition has increased and infant mortality has doubled.

ALTERNATIVES TO A HEARTLESS SYSTEM

It is hardly imaginable that anyone could knowingly devise such a ruthless, heartless system that is entirely devoted to increasing profit and largely indifferent to its human cost. This, however, is the system that is shaping life in Africa today, and it is the system that we must challenge. It is crucial that we do not accept the current academic wisdom that pretends that there are no choices or alternatives—a position one often hears rehearsed in

South Africa today. The debate has been conducted within the African National Congress (ANC), where opposing sides have adopted the labels TINA and THABA, standing for "there is no alternative" and "there has to be a better alternative."

Alternatives do exist. We have to challenge the assumption that structural adjustment is inevitably Africa's way to the future. A crucial condition is that African countries begin to cooperate with each other on a regional basis so that they are no longer forced to depend on the global structures and agencies that today try to dictate Africa's political and economic course. If this can happen, a better, more promising future can be envisaged.

What is certain is that we cannot accept the prospect of a world where the majority continues to become poorer and poorer while a few individuals continue to amass incredible riches. While the World Bank was celebrating its fiftieth birthday, demonstrators in the streets of Washington were declaring that "fifty years is enough!" They were part of a strong "Fifty Years Is Enough" campaign that has been mobilizing across the United States and other countries. . . .

They all understood what structural adjustment involves, and not just in the Third World, for this program is being carried out not only in Africa, Asia, and Latin America, but also in Canada and the United States. . . . People recognized that there is a link between the recolonization of Africa and other parts of the Third World, and the attack on workers' social and economic rights in the metropoles. They recognized the increasing homogenization of global rule as multinational corporations and multinational financial agencies such as the World Bank and the IMF increasingly control the economies of every country in the world. Most important, they recognized that the struggle for self-determination and human welfare must be a globally coordinated project. The future will decide whether this project can be realized. But there can be no doubt that the answer to this question will determine the course of African history in the twenty-first century.

"From 1990 to 1994, the United
States provided $13.6 billion . . .
of assistance to Africa. . . . These
assistance programs have played an
important role in promoting trade
and development."

FOREIGN AID PROMOTES AFRICAN DEVELOPMENT

George E. Moose

Africa receives billions of dollars of foreign aid from governments (including the United States), from multilateral financial
institutions such as the World Bank, and from private groups. In
the following viewpoint, George E. Moose argues that the foreign assistance provided by the United States and other sources
has been essential in helping to improve the economic performance and social development of African nations. He argues that
such aid should continue to be made available to African countries whose leaders promote private-sector growth and responsible economic and political strategies. A longtime official of the
United States Foreign Service, George E. Moose served as assistant secretary of state for African affairs from 1993 to 1997.

As you read, consider the following questions:

1. What signs of an economic turnaround in Africa does Moose
   describe?
2. What has the United States done to assist African countries,
   according to the author?
3. What three things does Moose list that need to be improved
   in supporting the economic development of Africa?

Excerpted from George E. Moose, "The Economic Situation in Sub-Saharan Africa," U.S.
Department of State Bulletin, August 12, 1996.

A frica is undergoing a major transformation. The clearest indicators of this transformation are the growth and expansion of democratic governments paralleled by significant economic reforms and liberalization. Africa's problems, however, remain daunting. Africa is the only region of the world where poverty is expected to increase during coming years. Too many African countries still struggle with civil strife, high population growth rates, an impoverished human resource base, large debt burdens, and minimal investment flows. Thirty-five of Sub-Saharan Africa's 48 countries are still classified as low income, with a per capita GNP of $700 or less in 1994. Twenty-eight countries are classified by the World Bank as severely indebted. Much of Africa is not fully integrated into the global economy; about one-third of the region's countries are not yet members of the World Trade Organization.

SIGNS OF RENEWED GROWTH

There are, however, many positive signs. Apart from a handful of countries experiencing civil unrest, most countries in the region are achieving at least a degree of progress toward sustained economic growth through more efficient use of resources. These positive signs offer hope about the future of Africa.

After four years of decline or stagnation, average real GDP growth in the region increased to 3.8% in 1995, the highest rate so far in the 1990s. That was also the first increase on a per capita basis (1.1%) since 1989. Growth also appears to be more widespread, exceeding 3% in nearly 30 countries. A number of reforming countries have recorded growth rates exceeding 4%. Botswana, Ghana, and Mauritius, among others, have been good performers.

While this is in part the result of higher commodity prices—which may be transitory—it also reflects the positive impact of more effective development programs, better economic policies, political transition in South Africa and other emerging democracies, and greater civil peace in some areas, all of which should make economic growth more sustainable. These gains would not have been possible without a firm commitment to economic and political reforms. While recent results are heartening, the progress is fragile and economic reform must be continued and deepened if it is to be sustained. . . .

SPECIAL PROGRAM OF ASSISTANCE

Economic performance in some 30 African countries has been boosted by the World Bank–coordinated Special Program of Assistance—SPA, launched in December 1987. The SPA brought together the World Bank, the International Monetary Fund (IMF), the African Development Bank, and bilateral donors in an effort to mobilize fast-disbursing assistance and to provide debt relief for countries adopting programs of stabilization and structural reform.

The most notable progress has been in liberalizing trade and foreign exchange regimes, and in most countries there also has been solid progress in reforming domestic markets. Several countries have undertaken parastatal reform and privatization, albeit much less rapidly and less completely than needed. Domestic-resource mobilization remains a problem in most countries. About half the SPA countries have made clear improvements in expenditure management, but stronger financial management remains important for all. More priority needs to be given to health, education, agriculture, and basic infrastructure. Public sector resource problems are complicated by low savings rates in nearly all parts of the continent.

The United Nations (UN) Special Initiative on Africa has identified debt relief as crucial to sustainable economic growth for Africa. The meeting of Group of Seven (G-7) leaders [of the world's leading industrial powers] reaffirmed the importance of supporting economic reform by urging action on multilateral debt and by supporting continued financing of an Enhanced Structural Adjustment Facility—ESAF. The United States has already provided extensive debt relief for Africa's poorest countries. In the early 1990s, we forgave over $1.1 billion in concessional debt for 19 of the poorest African countries implementing reforms. In addition, beginning in 1994, the United States joined other . . . governments in offering to reduce nonconcessional debt owed by the poorest, reforming countries. Finally, the United States has worked closely with the World Bank and the IMF to address the issue of multilateral debt. . . .

U.S. POLICY ACTIONS

From 1990 to 1994, the United States provided $13.6 billion— an average of $2.7 billion per year—of assistance to Africa, directly through the United States Agency for International Development (USAID) (including the PL 480 food assistance program) and indirectly through the World Bank and other international institutions. These assistance programs have played an important role in promoting trade and development. They must be continued. Ghana is an example of how U.S. support, including USAID's Trade and Investment Program, has yielded impressive results. Non-traditional exports increased significantly, including manufactured Afrocentric items for the U.S. market. At the same time, our exports to Ghana have increased.

The United States Information Agency (USIA) also plays a role in developing trade with Africa through a variety of programs which encourage the political, social, and economic climates necessary for increased trade and investment. In 1996, 270 African entrepreneurs will visit the United States as part of USIA's exchange and visitor programs. Young African entrepreneurs and business people will intern in American companies in the United States while U.S. lecturers and researchers will teach and work in Africa, explaining the advantages of free-market economics. USIA programs in Ghana and Nigeria help develop business associations there.

An Impressive Record

There has been an impressive turnaround in the recent track record of U.S. assistance to Africa. Today, most American resources are directed to those African countries dedicated to political and economic reform, and with the best prospects for expanded trade and investment. Among the leading recipients of U.S. aid are South Africa, Uganda, Ghana, Ethiopia, Mozambique, and Mali—all of which have shown significant political progress after long periods of conflict and/or stagnation, and have open and growing markets. American assistance is contributing significantly to their success.

David F. Gordon and Howard Wolpe, *World Policy Journal*, Spring 1998.

During the past three decades, there have been a number of approaches to development. The conclusion to be drawn from this experience is that development needs balance—the development stool has several legs. There are several things that donors are doing well. We need to retain support for macroeconomic reform—that is the basis for the rest. We also must continue capacity-building and human resource development, with particular attention to the education of women. If we forget these basics, we are in trouble.

There are other things that have not been done as well—that need to be improved:

• There should be a stronger focus on the role of trade and investment and on strengthening the African private sector as the engine of growth.

• We encourage increased regional economic integration in Africa in order to achieve economies of scale necessary to attract investment. There has been much talk of the importance of this, but progress has been more limited.

• We need better ways to coordinate and collaborate among donors. There have been improvements, but more must be done to use declining resources to the best effect.

To ensure continued progress, African governments and international donors must use all resources efficiently. In this era of declining donor resources, wise stewardship of available funds is a top priority. Realistically, we cannot expect an increase in overall donor resources, including from the United States. However, the United States is committed to working with African governments and other donors to direct our resources where they can make the most difference.

Nevertheless, foreign aid from the U.S. and other donors could not begin to finance rapid economic growth on the continent. Most of the capital needed to finance rapid growth must come from the private sectors, both within Africa and abroad, including flight capital. Continued program lending to support economic reforms remains important. However, where economic reform has produced the necessary stability in external accounts and fiscal balances, scarce development dollars can be directed to the highest development priorities. . . .

CREATING AN ENABLING ENVIRONMENT

The UN Special Initiative states that "donor-led development is not a credible option." We concur. Increasing and sustaining the rate of growth enough to reduce poverty requires African ownership of the development program. This must be widespread. Governments must strive to muster support from groups benefiting from reforms.

African leaders now must shoulder the responsibility of furthering economic liberalization, developing enduring institutions, mobilizing domestic resources, forging dynamic partnerships with the private sector, protecting the environment, and promoting regional alliances. African leaders have largely abandoned the practice of blaming others for their troubles; instead, to a remarkable degree, they have become brutally honest in examining their policy shortcomings. In our bilateral assistance, we are talking more and more with the "stakeholders" and are pleased with their increasing focus on African ownership of the development process.

The task for African governments is to create an enabling environment for private sector growth by removing constraints to political and economic freedom and encouraging greater individual participation. Investors expect good governance. This means:

1. Decentralized political activity;
2. Accountable and responsible government; and
3. Respect for human rights, including a free press that permits a free and open exchange of ideas.

Investors also expect access to a transparent, predictable legal system to enforce contracts and resolve disputes.

USIA's programming in support of free media, civic education, and democratic institutions is helping to establish the political and social underpinnings for economic reform and growth. This work includes programs in Burkina Faso, Malawi, Mali, Niger, Senegal, Tanzania, Zambia, and Zimbabwe aimed at helping private radio and television stations become financially viable, as well as journalism training programs which promote competitive, independent media and reduced ethnic tensions.

USAID is also working with many of these governments to help them in the process of creating an enabling environment more conducive to economic growth; however, its capacity to deepen and broaden these programs is limited by the fact that USAID's overall budget is constrained. . . .

THE WAY FORWARD

Our development assistance cannot solve every problem. It is no substitute for good government and cannot make up for failed economic policies, but it can make a decisive difference in promoting opportunities for prosperity, democracy, and stability around the world. We have learned many lessons about what works and what does not, and we are generally applying them well.

Our assistance to Africa must be maintained, especially when so many African countries, from Mozambique to Sierra Leone, are making quiet progress in stabilizing their economies and building democracies. Further cuts to our aid programs would not just sacrifice ideals Americans support; they would hinder American efforts to strengthen governments which share our views. . . .

There are many positive signs of economic growth and increasing economic and political freedom on the continent. We believe that through increased cooperation and more efficient use of available resources we can help further Africa's positive transformation.

> "While ... foreign aid suffers countless problems, its structural flaws, crippling preconditions, and self-perpetuating tendencies remain the most significant."

FOREIGN AID HINDERS AFRICAN DEVELOPMENT

Isaias Afwerki

Isaias Afwerki is the president of Eritrea, a country in northeast Africa that became formally independent of Ethiopia in 1993. In the following viewpoint, he argues that foreign aid offered to Eritrea and other African countries often comes with too many conditions and rules imposed by donor nations. Foreign aid programs are often self-perpetuating and serve the interests of donors instead of the intended beneficiaries. Afwerki concludes that foreign aid, if it is to help Africa, must be completely re-structured so as to emphasize African development goals and self-sufficiency.

As you read, consider the following questions:

1. What kinds of preconditions to foreign aid offers does Afwerki describe?
2. What should be the yardstick for measuring the effectiveness of foreign aid programs, according to the author?
3. What past example of a successful foreign aid initiative does Afwerki mention?

Reprinted from Isaias Afwerki, "Foreign Aid Works Best When It's Self-Limiting," *Forum for Applied Research and Public Policy*, Winter 1997, with permission.

Early in 1992, only a few months after Eritrea's long war of liberation from Ethiopia ended, we received a high-level mission from a friendly country determined to help us make the difficult political and social transition to peace and salvage our devastated economy.

STRINGS ATTACHED

Although the offer was well-intentioned, the package of food and commodity aid was woefully inadequate for addressing our huge needs. Yet that was not the reason we felt compelled to politely decline the offer. The real problem was that the aid package arrived with an appalling number of strings attached, chiefly those associated with privatization of Eritrea's public enterprises. In fact, the donor nation stipulated that the $17 million in commodity aid would be disbursed in several stages, over a three-year period. Each disbursement would be contingent on Eritrea's success in selling a strict number of public enterprises.

The most troubling aspect of this proposed arrangement was that the donor nation didn't even bother to conduct a cursory analysis to determine whether there were potential buyers—either foreign or domestic—who might be interested in purchasing these businesses. Nor did it investigate the government's official policy regarding privatization efforts.

In January 1997, we received a mission from another country that expressed interest in supporting Eritrea's energy and education programs. I was amazed to learn that this support would hinge on whether the "government had taken quantifiable measures in various sectors to meet women empowerment targets" recommended at the Beijing Conference on Women held in 1995.

The mission went further and requested proof from the National Union of Eritrean Women that government restructuring of the civil service, which had been largely implemented in three phases since 1994, had made "special provisions for women on the grounds of gender equality."

This condition, which would have contradicted the policies of other donors, including the International Monetary Fund, was apparently made without any knowledge or scrutiny of our nation's overall policy of affirmative action aimed at promoting the long-term equality of both genders.

Though these two instances do not necessarily reflect the overall status of international aid programs, they do underscore the policy fragmentation and chaos that would ensue if nations were to comply with such heavy-handed prescriptions. They are also useful in informing the debate on the very objectives of foreign aid and the necessity of fostering sustainable, indigenous economic development.

EVALUATING FOREIGN AID

Indeed, the only yardstick for measuring the viability, effectiveness, and desirability of foreign aid, in the form of grants or concessions, is the extent to which it enables the beneficiaries to gradually reach the point where they no longer need it. Indeed, foreign aid works best when it becomes obsolete, rather than self-perpetuating.

Evidence suggests that aid may be having the opposite effect. In fact, aid's overall effectiveness has been substantially eroded by the flaws in its structure and by the innumerable conditions, rules, and procedures imposed by donor nations.

In short, if foreign aid is expected to inject much-needed financial capital, facilitate the transfer of skill and knowledge, introduce innovative production techniques, and build local capacity in the recipient countries, the pattern on the ground suggests that aid is falling short of these ambitious goals.

HANDOUTS VS. HELPING HANDS

In many instances, excessive "donor" involvement in aid management has not only reduced the effectiveness and efficiency of aid by delaying timely implementation, but it has also limited local involvement and capacity building because foreign consultants and experts tend to take on the majority of the administrative work.

Consider, for instance, that conservative estimates place the number of foreign experts administering aid in Africa today in excess of 100,000. This figure says much about the tendency of aid programs to create self-perpetuating circumstances.

Moreover, the seemingly endless number of missions to assess project feasibility before projects are launched, not to mention costly mid-term reviews, often entail considerable expenses that could have been funneled into productive activities to benefit the recipient nations.

Though international aid programs show tremendous room for improvement, my intention is not to reinforce isolationist pundits in Washington and other Western capitals who think "foreign aid has become a rat hole" that should be plugged. But how can we reconcile that jaundiced view of international aid with trends toward increased globalization and interdependence?

The pitfalls of isolationism are obvious; the idea that one can live safely and comfortably within the confines of one's territory while a substantial portion of humanity remains in the grips of endemic poverty is an illusion. Indeed, growing affluence and consumerism in one part of the globe cannot coexist for long with extreme deprivation in another part of the same planet without threatening world peace and security.

FOREIGN AID AND NATIONAL INTEREST

Historically, foreign aid has not always been predicated on a sense of altruism and human solidarity but instead focused on concerns over national interest. The threat of instability caused by increased poverty is much more pronounced in the context of the global village of the 21st century, where national borders come to mean less and less.

The threat to international peace and security posed by terrorism, which in the final analysis is fueled by deprivation and economic frustration, serves as a lesson in this regard.

But how can we strike a balance between focused, self-limiting aid intended to help recipient nations rise to their feet versus the disabling and self-perpetuating assistance intended to boost the donor nations' sense of security?

THE AID BUSINESS

What is the point of aid in Africa? Is it really to benefit Africans, or is it a new form of imperialism? Perhaps it was originally intended as a humanitarian option, an apology for decades of colonial pillage. But it has now become a multibillion-dollar, self-perpetuating industry with a bloated, inefficient, and often corrupt bureaucracy that more often than not causes, rather than alleviates, environmental and social disasters. . . .

Of course, the aid business has no desire to see itself phased out. There are an estimated 80,000–100,000 expatriate aid "experts" in Africa alone, excluding short-stay consultants. They live the good life, with cars, money, and housing. Conservatively, an "expert" will earn $100,000 a year. Nearly half the money budgeted as "aid" for Africa is spent on salaries and perks for the "experts," and most of the rest goes to finance the bureaucracies. Very little trickles down to the poor. And many of the "experts" have little clue about the job they are supposed to be doing.

Tony Weaver, *World Press Review*, July 1997.

In my view, nothing less than a total overhaul of the existing aid system will do. The endless conditions, provisos, and inflexible rules that are part of most current aid packages must give way to initiatives based on partnerships and shared ownership. To that end, we must replace the very words "donor" and "recipient" by new terms that reflect a sense of symmetric partnership.

Some might argue, with a certain degree of justification, that there is no novelty in this approach, as the concept is becoming increasingly common in the vocabulary of many Western nations. To the extent that partnerships are pursued in good faith, it is an auspicious beginning. But they will require much encouragement; old habits die hard, and the resistance to change engendered by the forces of inertia will be significant.

SUSTAINABLE AID POLICY

Even if all partners in aid were to fully adopt these reforms, the changes will be worthless if they fail to create an environment in which aid brings recipient nations to a point where they can fend for themselves and the aid becomes redundant. The most crucial issue that must be addressed, therefore, is the sustainability of aid and the extent to which it is structurally embedded in the development policy of the country on the receiving end.

In this regard, foreign aid must be carefully designed to be focused and nonpermanent. In my view, a symmetric partnership can never be built on the basis of an exchange that is permanently skewed. The goal of foreign aid must be to create an environment that will transform the relationship into a mutually beneficial interaction of trade and investment.

I do not believe this is an impossible task, even in situations of great adversity. Indeed, there have been cases in the past in which massive and purposeful intervention was successful. One example that comes to mind is the United States' support of Europe in the aftermath of World War II. Whether Africa can summon geopolitical considerations of this magnitude amidst the political realities of the 21st century is, of course, a different matter.

And while the Eritrean government welcomes properly focused aid programs, it is inclined to discourage the proliferation of fragmented aid programs that do a better job of meeting the needs of donor, rather than recipient, nations.

While the milieu of foreign aid suffers countless problems, its structural flaws, crippling preconditions, and self-perpetuating tendencies remain the most significant. These deficiencies must be corrected if, through foreign aid, we hope to address economic imbalances and promote a more egalitarian global village.

| "Over the last six years, 38 million people in sub-Saharan Africa have sunk further into poverty due to their governments' international debt."

AFRICA NEEDS GREATER DEBT RELIEF FROM FOREIGN CREDITORS

Veronica Brand

A significant controversy surrounding African economic development is the continent's external debt to private lenders, foreign governments, and multilateral institutions such as the World Bank and the International Monetary Fund (IMF). Such debt in sub-Saharan Africa has grown from $3 billion in 1962 to about $225 billion in 1998. Many African countries spend more in debt repayments than they do for education and social welfare programs. In the following viewpoint, Veronica Brand argues that debt obligations pose a significant obstacle to African nations struggling to develop their economies, and that creditors should consider forgiving some of Africa's debt. Debt repayment programs imposed by the IMF and World Bank create special hardships for Africa's poorest citizens, she contends. Brand, a citizen of the African country of Zimbabwe, lives in Rome where she is general councilor and treasurer of a religious order.

As you read, consider the following questions:

1. How much does each person in the Third World owe to the West, according to Brand?
2. How have Zimbabwe's education and health programs been affected by debt concerns, according to the author?
3. According to Brand, what problems exist with the Heavily Indebted Poor Countries (HIPC) initiative?

Reprinted from Veronica Brand, "The Poor Pay Twice for the Third World's Debts," *Los Angeles Times*, November 5, 1997, by permission of the *Los Angeles Times*.

World Bank President James Wolfensohn told the institution's 1997 annual meeting that the "challenge of inclusion is the key development challenge of our time." Although Wolfensohn acknowledged the need to reduce the disparities across and within countries as an economic and moral imperative many questions remain.

Over the last six years since 1991, 38 million people in sub-Saharan Africa have sunk further into poverty due to their governments' international debt and the structural adjustment programs imposed by international financial institutions.

What Debt Means in Human Terms

In human terms, this means that each person in the Third World owes about $420 to the West. Joao, a boy selling oranges in the interior of Mozambique, would need to sell 4,400 baskets of oranges to repay his share of the debt. The woman selling her crochet work at a Zimbabwean roadside market would need to produce and sell 100 hand-crocheted bedspreads. The teacher in Zambia would have to pay 14 months of her salary. The technical expert who comes to Africa on a development mission often earns that amount in a single day. What does inclusion mean when such discrepancies exist?

Poor people are further impoverished by macroeconomic policies, collectively known as structural adjustments, that their government adopts as conditions for further borrowing and debt rescheduling from the International Monetary Fund and World Bank. The United Nations Children's Fund (UNICEF) and the International Labor Organization document that the cost of structural adjustments is borne disproportionately by the poor and their children. So when aid and debt relief are made conditional on rigid structural adjustment measures that intensify and spread poverty, then the poor have paid twice.

In Zimbabwe, the structural adjustment program forced the reintroduction of school fees and charges for basic health services. These "cost recovery" measures are linked by independent monitoring groups to drops in school attendance, especially for girls. In the two years after structural adjustments were introduced, health spending was cut by one-third, . . . maternity clinic visits fell and the number of women dying in childbirth doubled.

Structural adjustments also led to the removal of subsidies on basic foodstuffs, raising food prices beyond the reach of many poor families and leaving them without proper nutrition. Other economic reforms caused a flood of cheap imports, leading to the collapse of some small local industries. The explosion of child labor is directly linked to structural adjustments as more children are drawn into the informal economy to supplement family incomes. Wage freezes and retrenchments in the formal sector have placed more burden on poor women in the informal economy, where they become by default the principal bread-winners of their families.

THE HIPC INITIATIVE

The much publicized Heavily Indebted Poor Countries (HIPC) initiative is one strategy introduced by the IMF and World Bank to address Third World debt. While acclaimed as an important policy shift, it fails to address the problems of people like Joao and the conditions that threaten the welfare and dignity of millions of people like him. The $5 billion to $7 billion that the HIPC initiative provides—roughly what U.S. citizens spend annually on athletic shoes—is only 5% of the debt of the 20% of countries most likely to qualify.

Delays in implementing the HIPC initiative, due largely to a lack of political will from northern governments like the U.S., exact a steep price from the poorest in the southern world. Oxfam [a development agency] estimates that in Uganda, the one-year delay in debt relief will cost six times the total government spending on health care. Mozambique—which will not qualify for debt relief until 2002—will spend $240 million in debt service this year as compared with only $144 million on its post-war reconstruction.

THE CONSEQUENCES OF DEBT

In Britain there would be an outcry if the Government were to introduce charges for education, leave children without desks and roofs on their classrooms, or let hospitals and clinics run out of basic drugs. In the developing world, it happens every day of every year, as money is siphoned off to pay debts. . . .

In Africa as a whole, one out of every two children does not go to school, but governments spend four times more in debt payments to northern creditors than they spend on health and education.

Larry Elliott, *The Guardian*, May 11, 1998.

Unless we recognize that international debt touches peoples' lives directly, debt will remain a point of academic debate—not a moral imperative. This is why a growing number of religious organizations are calling for debt relief as an urgent matter of justice. They recognize that the debt trap is economically unsustainable and morally unacceptable. From an economic perspective, maintaining the debt neglects long-term development strategies aimed at poverty reduction. From a moral perspective, the backlog of unpayable debt is an unjustifiable burden on those who suffer most from obligations they did not choose to assume.

Unsustainable debt in the poorest nations is a new form of slavery that keeps current and future generations chained in dehumanizing poverty. Addressing it requires bold action and prophetic solutions.

Former Tanzanian President Julius Nyerere once asked "Must we starve our children to pay our debts?" The call to forgive unsustainable debt is not a plea for charity, it is a cry for justice. The challenge of "inclusion" will not be met until the U.S. and other industrialized nations have the political will to implement policies that promote equitable global relationships.

"The HIPC initiative . . . gives the
international community a way to
marry debt relief with the
encouragement of policies that will
ensure that the relief achieves
poverty reduction."

AFRICA HAS SUFFICIENT DEBT RELIEF

Jack Boorman

Jack Boorman is director of policy development for the International Monetary Fund (IMF), a United Nations specialized agency that has loaned out billions of dollars to African nations. Some people and organizations in Africa and elsewhere have campaigned for significantly reducing and even cancelling Africa's foreign debt to the IMF and other institutions, arguing that the money used for debt repayment should instead go towards education, health, and other social development programs. Boorman argues that the IMF has provided adequate debt forgiveness through its 1996 Heavily Indebted Poor Countries (HIPC) initiative that targets special debt relief for countries that take significant steps to restructure their economies. He also rebuts several claims made about the debt issue, arguing that foreign debt does not cause poverty and that debt relief is no panacea for developing countries.

As you read, consider the following questions:

1. What connection exists between debt and social spending, according to Boorman?
2. Why would cancelling the debt of the poorest countries fail to improve people's lives, in the author's view?
3. According to Boorman, what have been the accomplishments of the HIPC initiative?

M uch has been written about the initiative for the heavily indebted poor countries since its launch in 1996 by the International Monetary Fund (IMF) and the World Bank. I would like to debunk some of the myths that have surfaced, on debt relief in general and the Heavily Indebted Poor Countries (HIPC) initiative in particular.

The first is that widespread poverty in the HIPCs is due to debt. While the explanations of poverty are diverse, the prime causes of poverty and of misuse of loans are inappropriate economic policies, poor lending decisions by creditors and social and political disruptions. Many deeply poor countries do not have large debts. Thus the elimination of debt without the adoption of appropriate economic policies would do little to eradicate poverty.

As many African countries have improved their policies— often with IMF support—the economic outlook for Africa has brightened: real output has been growing at between 4% and 5%, and finally per capita incomes are beginning to rise.

DEBT AND SOCIAL SPENDING

The second myth is that debt is responsible for insufficient social spending. In reality, debt does not preclude any of the HIPCs from providing basic social services. So why do critics conclude it does? The devil is in the detail: critics often compare scheduled debt service with social spending levels. But this recognizes neither the debt relief provided nor the much higher inflows of foreign aid.

A look at the HIPCs from 1993 to 1997 shows that: actual debt service paid was, on average, only about two-thirds of scheduled debt service, and much lower in some of the poorest countries; actual debt service paid in most HIPCs was lower than government budgetary outlays on health and education; and foreign financing was on average twice debt service paid and in some HIPCs much higher.

PROBLEMS CAUSED BY DEBT RELIEF

The third myth is that "wiping the slate clean"—writing off poorest countries' debt—would prove a panacea. But in reality a total and unconditional write-off would pose more problems than it would solve—and what guarantee is there that the money saved would be put to effective use?

Indeed, unconditional cancellation risks debt relief being squandered. This could further erode support for aid flows in developed countries, which are already at an historic low. Moreover, such debt cancellation would be difficult to justify, particularly to countries which are poor but not heavily indebted.

THE HIPC INITIATIVE

The HIPC initiative, by contrast, gives the international community a way to marry debt relief with the encouragement of policies that will ensure that the relief achieves poverty reduction.

The initiative is designed to provide comprehensive debt relief to the poorest countries, encourage private sector-led growth, empower poor people and reduce poverty. It is also to promote health and education outlays and encourage continued aid flows—vital given the dependence of HIPCs on such inflows.

Critics of the HIPC initiative might do better to concentrate on those who deny the basic need for increased resource transfers from the better-off to the poorer countries. On this, we could quickly join forces.

So where do we stand now? In the two years since the launch of the initiative, commitments of more than $6 billion (£3.6 billion) in debt service relief have been made to Bolivia, Burkina Faso, Cote d'Ivoire, Guyana, Mali, Mozambique, and Uganda—not exactly a demonstration of a lack of political will. Over the coming year [1999], we hope to consider a number of others, including Ethiopia and Mauritania.

DEBT RELIEF NO PANACEA

[The] implication that a total debt write-off will prove a panacea for Africa is sadly mistaken. . . .

Unconditional cancellation could risk debt relief being squandered on corruption, military expenditure, or grandiose projects with little, if any, benefit in terms of sustainable growth or poverty reduction.

G.E. Gondwe, *Financial Times*, August 26, 1998.

The fourth myth for debunking is that debt relief takes too long. But HIPCs receive considerable debt relief and new financing early in the process. Countries are asked to establish a six-year track record of good economic performance under World Bank and IMF-supported programmes, with decisions on debt relief made after the first three years.

Of the seven countries for which assistance has been committed, six will receive debt relief after a second stage of less than three years, and for three, this period will be only one year.

The claim that the adjustment period is unduly long ignores the reality of the problems faced by HIPCs and the time needed to tackle these problems.

Our objective is speedy implementation of the HIPC initiative. It is our hope that HIPCs will seize this unique opportunity to exit, once and for all, from the debt rescheduling process and lay the foundation for sustainable, pro-poor growth.

PERIODICAL BIBLIOGRAPHY

The following articles have been selected to supplement the diverse views presented in this chapter. Addresses are provided for periodicals not indexed in the *Readers' Guide to Periodical Literature*, the *Alternative Press Index*, the *Social Sciences Index*, or the *Index to Legal Periodicals and Books*.

Daniel Mensah Brande	"Kill or Cure," *New Internationalist*, January/February 1997.
Deborah Bräutigam	"Economic Takeoff in Africa?" *Current History*, May 1998.
Economist	"Emerging Africa," June 14, 1997.
David F. Gordon and Howard Wolpe	"The Other Africa: An End to Afro-Pessimism," *World Policy Journal*, Spring 1998.
Sonya Huber	"Debt-Free Jubilee," *In These Times*, December 13, 1998.
Jesse L. Jackson Jr.	"HOPE for Africa," *Nation*, March 1, 1999.
Stefan Lovgren	"Instead of Aid, Trade," *U.S. News & World Report*, October 13, 1997.
Michael Maren	"The Faces of Famine," *Newsweek*, July 27, 1998.
Richard C. Morais	"Africa: The Untold Story," *Forbes*, November 17, 1997.
Nation	"African Trade-Offs," April 6, 1998.
Ann Pettifor	"The Economic Bondage of Debt—and the Birth of a New Movement," *New Left Review*, July/August 1998.
Ken Wells	"Microcredit Arrives in Africa, but Can It Match Asian Success?" *Wall Street Journal*, September 29, 1998.
Mark Whitaker	"Mean Streets," *New Internationalist*, January/February 1997.

CHAPTER 2

WHAT POLICIES CAN BEST FOSTER PEACE IN AFRICA?

Chapter Preface

In April 1994, Juvénal Habyarimana, the president of the central African nation of Rwanda, was returning from peace negotiations that promised a halt to civil war with the rebel Rwandan Patriotic Front (RPF) when his plane was shot down by assailants yet unknown. His death provoked a period of horrific ethnic violence in the nation historically divided between the Hutu and Tutsi ethnic groups. Over the next several months an estimated 800,000 Rwandans—mostly Tutsis—were massacred in what most observers now agree was a genocidal campaign orchestrated by elements within the Hutu-dominated Rwandan government and armed forces. By July 1994, the RPF, which was led by Tutsis, had successfully seized control of the country, causing over a million Hutus to flee to Zaire and Tanzania. They settled in enormous and squalid refugee camps where supplies were inadequate and diseases such as cholera were common. By August 1994 an estimated one quarter of the pre-war population of Rwanda was dead or in exile.

Apportioning blame for this train of events has caused some disagreement. Some observers argue that the underlying cause was longstanding hostility between the Tutsis and Hutus. Others argue that the two groups have lived together in relative peace for centuries (some question whether they should even be categorized as separate ethnic groups), but that divisions between the Hutus and Tutsis were enflamed (if not created) by Rwanda's Belgian colonial rulers in the twentieth century. Many people have criticized the international community and the United Nations for failing to do more to prevent the 1994 events.

While Rwanda is perhaps the most extreme case of conflict in Africa, it is far from the only one on the continent. Over the past several decades Africa has been rent by numerous wars, border disputes, rebellions, and civil disturbances. In addition to Rwanda, at least six other conflicts—in Angola, Ethiopia, Mozambique, Somalia, Sudan, and Uganda—have taken at least a half million lives. Some of the conflicts are between nations, while many occur within national borders. The viewpoints in the following chapter examine various proposals to manage conflict in Africa and prevent a repetition of the 1994 tragic events in Rwanda.

"African countries have to put in place a reliable . . . conflict management mechanism . . . that can swiftly respond to conflicts anywhere in the continent."

THE ORGANIZATION OF AFRICAN UNITY CAN REDUCE CONFLICT

Amadu Sesay

Amadu Sesay is a professor of international relations at the Obafemi Awolowo University in Ile-Ife, Nigeria. In the following viewpoint, he examines the prospects of regional organizations in Africa—especially the Organization of African Unity (OAU)—for preventing and managing conflict. The end of the cold war between the United States and the Soviet Union, he contends, presents new opportunities for African nations to manage their own affairs and work for peace on the continent. However, the conflict-management initiatives of the OAU, which was founded in 1963, are hampered by a lack of funding and reluctance on the part of African countries to interfere in internal conflicts of other nations. Sesay concludes that African nations must, through the OAU or some other agency, cooperate to create a peacekeeping force and other mechanisms to intervene and respond to political turmoil, border clashes, and other conflicts in Africa.

As you read, consider the following questions:
1. What are the debilitating effects of conflict on Africa's development, in Sesay's opinion?
2. How has the OAU's experience in peacekeeping in Chad affected subsequent actions, according to Sesay?

Excerpted from Amadu Sesay, "Regional and Sub-Regional Conflict Management Efforts," in *Africa in the Post–Cold War International System*, edited by Sola Akinrinade and Amadu Sesay (London: Pinter, 1998).

The fall of the Berlin Wall in 1989, which signalled the end of East-West ideological rivalry and the threat of nuclear confrontation between the superpowers [the Soviet Union and the United States], gave rise to much optimism that the world was entering a new era. The envisaged era was one that would bring a peace dividend, in particular peace between and within nations, an era when conflicts that had been promoted by the Cold War environment would be resolved peacefully at the 'peace table'. It was widely expected that the period would usher in political stability and economic development, especially in peripheries like Africa.

AFRICA AND THE END OF THE COLD WAR

However, the euphoria was short-lived. In 1993, for example, there were 52 conflicts in 42 countries. . . . In Africa, the end of the Cold War seriously compounded the continent's security dilemma in several important ways. Part of the problem lies in the fact that the post–Cold War international order abolished 'political protégés', which had hitherto been protected by the superpowers. Many dissidents, who were held in check by the prospect of Great Power intervention on the side of 'constituted' authorities, were emboldened by the withdrawal of superpower support to bid openly for political power in many states. Not surprisingly, the continent was in 1992 declared the most violent, and in 1993, it accounted for 11 of the 26 major conflicts in the world.

One distinguishing feature of post–Cold War conflicts in Africa is that they are mainly within states. Many are also the result of long years of cultural, political, religious and ethnic marginalization and domination, as already pointed out. The new world order, it is obvious, brought in its wake a great deal of disorder in Africa. . . .

Not surprisingly, post–Cold War conflicts have led to humanitarian emergencies and tragedies. Millions of people are forced to flee to neighbouring states as refugees, while millions more are displaced within their states. With over 6 million affected, Africa has the largest refugee population in the world. Globally, the refugee population is also on the increase. According to the United Nations High Commission for Refugees (UNHCR), 'in 1970, there were only 2.5 million; in 1980, 11 million; and in 1993, more than 16 million'. . . .

On the whole, post–Cold War conflicts have had a debilitating impact on Africa's collective psyche, socio-economic development and political development. They have not been susceptible to conventional modes of conflict management by sub-regional and regional organizations or even the UN. The rest of this viewpoint examines post–Cold War conflict management efforts in Africa, and suggests ways of avoiding and/or resolving African conflicts effectively, in the 1990s and beyond.

REGIONAL CONFLICT MANAGEMENT EFFORTS

The development of a conflict avoidance and conflict resolution capability by regional or sub-regional agencies like the Organization of African Unity (OAU) and the Economic Community of West African States (ECOWAS) was designed to give practical expression to the concept of 'try Africa first'. Both during and after the Cold War, 'try Africa first' was justified in several ways. It was designed to ward off superpower and/or Great Power intrusion into the continent, by giving African states the first option to find solutions to inter- or intra-state conflicts in the continent. Unarguably, then, the concept is in line with the UN Charter, which recognizes the role of regional agencies in the maintenance of world peace and security. Regional and sub-regional conflict management initiatives confirm the fact that they do possess certain attributes and advantages which the global UN lacks: their local experience, local expertise and geopolitical proximity, which make them ideal instruments, at least in theory, for managing conflicts within and between members.

It is in the individual and collective interests of African states in both the short and the long term to manage and/or resolve conflicts in their continent. . . . In the post–Cold War era, 'try Africa first' is relevant because of the increasing political and economic marginalization of the continent. With the attention of the Western powers focused on the former Soviet satellites in Eastern Europe, and Russia itself, the onus is on Africans to find effective multilateral solutions to their problems, at both regional and sub-regional levels. . . .

PAST ACTIONS OF THE OAU

One of the major reasons for creating the OAU in 1963 was the desire by the newly independent states to maintain peace and harmony among themselves. The move was informed by the realization that the post-colonial states were very disparate and fragile political formations which could be easily destabilized. In addition, the enormous task of nation-building called for some modicum of order and predictability in inter-state relations. Not surprisingly, the fundamental principles of the OAU upheld the sovereign equality of the new states, and barred members from interfering in the domestic affairs of one another. The Charter also unreservedly condemned all forms of subversion and assassination by member states. These principles were meant to deter states, especially the powerful ones, from meddling in the affairs of weaker members.

The founding fathers created an elaborate conflict management machinery in the Commission on Mediation, Arbitration, and Conciliation. Unfortunately, the Commission anticipated conflicts which had no bearing on the realities on the ground, so it was never used. First, the consent of members had to be sought before the Commission could commence its work, which was not possible, as members jealously guarded their newly won political independence. Second was the legalistic approach of the Commission to African conflicts. Many African leaders were wary of using the Commission because they detested arbitration. As one official in the OAU Secretariat put it, 'African leaders were scared of appearing before judges that could be young enough to be their grandchildren.' Another reason was the possibility of going through a long and expensive judicial process whose outcome they could not predict. Finally, the very political nature of most African conflicts at this time precluded the use of the Commission, which was eventually dismantled in 1977. From then on, the OAU relied on *ad hoc* devices to manage conflict between and within its members.

Among these 'new' devices was the Good Offices Committee, which is usually made up of prominent leaders or statesmen. Their usual task is to investigate the issues in dispute and to use their prestige and standing to bring the parties to the conference table, with a view to settling their differences amicably. There was also what became popularly known as 'Presidential Mediation': a strategy which involved the use in conflict management of experienced African heads of state noted for their wisdom, neutrality or age. . . .

By far the most audacious attempt at conflict management and resolution by the OAU was its [1981–1982] peacekeeping mission in Chad, a largely *ad hoc* arrangement, as the Charter made no provision for a peacekeeping force. Unfortunately, the mission was an unqualified failure. . . . With the failure of the Chad mission, the OAU and its members suffered a serious psychological defeat and setback from which they are yet to recover fully. The collapse of the first indigenous peacekeeping operation was seen as a humiliation for the OAU, not only by members, but also by external observers and supporters. Thus, the OAU suffered a crushing blow to both its prestige and its salience in

Chad. The debacle, above all, cast serious doubts on the OAU's ability to play effectively the role of a conflict manager in Africa. In other words, the Chad episode provided a test case in terms of the ability and capacity of African states, through their continental organization, to defuse a conflict situation successfully and to legitimize the concept of 'try Africa first'. To that extent, the OAU was effectively disarmed in Chad, and its self-confidence was left severely, if not irreparably, dented. For individual African states, the successful take-over of N'djamena [Chad's capital] by [rebel leader] Hissène Habré in June 1982 [despite the presence of an OAU peacekeeping force, which was subsequently withdrawn as Chad's civil war continued] brought to the fore the dangers inherent in the local management of a complicated domestic conflict in a Cold War environment. Accordingly, 'try Africa first' as an approach to conflict management failed woefully in Chad. And with that, many states were forced to resort to the old, tried and rather effective insurance policy: relying on bilateral arrangements with either the former colonial masters or the Cold War superpowers for their local security needs.

AFRICA'S IMPERATIVE

As the twenty-first century approaches, the imperative for Africa to take a hard look at the scourge of conflicts and to design viable mechanisms for conflict resolution and management capacities becomes more pressing. Put most simply, for Africa to remain relevant in the new international order, the peoples of Africa, through their continental political body, the Organization of African Unity (OAU), must fill the vacuum left by Cold War engagements.

Chris J. Bakweshega, *Out of Conflict—From War to Peace in Africa*, 1998.

The OAU played only a limited role in managing African conflicts in the Cold War era. Among the reasons responsible for its poor record are a weak institutional base and the obvious *ad hoc* nature of the strategies, which tended to make them poor 'fire brigade' operations. Furthermore, success depended to a large extent not only on the nature of the conflict to be managed or resolved but also on the disposition of the parties in conflict, and sometimes even that of the superpowers. Another limitation was the restraint imposed by the principle of non-interference in the domestic affairs of other states which OAU members subscribed to. For instance, throughout the long war between Ethiopia and Eritrea, the OAU maintained an embarrassing silence. . . . The OAU also kept quiet throughout the long reign of terror of the 'three tyrants' in the 1970s: Idi Amin in Uganda, Jean-Bédel Bokassa in the Central African Republic and Macias Nguema in Equatorial Guinea. In fact, the 1975 OAU summit took place in Uganda under the chairmanship of Idi Amin, even as he was committing gross human rights violations in his country. . . . It was not uncommon in this period, then, to hear intellectuals and other observers of African politics describing the OAU as a 'toothless bulldog.'

A New Role

The end of the Cold War left the OAU in search of a new role and relevance within and outside the continent. Many of the issues that made the OAU relevant to its members in the Cold War era, such as decolonization and apartheid, are no longer on the agenda of pan-African summits. However, with the unprecedented wave of violent intra-state conflict that swept across the continent following the collapse of communism in the 1990s, conflict management became an issue to which the OAU was forced to turn its attention.

There are compelling reasons why the OAU and sub-regional organizations in Africa tried to be involved in conflict avoidance, management and resolution efforts in post–Cold War Africa. Conflicts are an unnecessary drain on scarce resources, especially at a time when the Great Powers are withdrawing from the continent. . . . There is clearly a direct link between economic development, democracy and conflicts in Africa. . . . Finally, an argument can be made that conflict is itself contagious. Consequently:

> the security and stability of each African country is linked to that of its neighbours. . . . One country cannot enjoy peace by itself like an island in a sea of insecurity and conflict. Instability along the borders precipitates tensions and military deployments with the risk of armed confrontation, and gives rise to refugees who in turn cross national borders, and could pose security threats to host states.

[address by OAU secretary-general Salim Ahmed Salim, 1991]

Constraints on the OAU

Nevertheless, the OAU has been reluctant to get actively involved in post–Cold War conflict management efforts. A major reason for this is that the new conflicts are not easily susceptible to conventional conflict management methods. Many of them are classified as internal; these include civil wars, protracted civil strife and even state collapse. Furthermore, after its disastrous performance in Chad, as already mentioned, the OAU is not psychologically ready and does not possess the political will to try peacekeeping again. This is in spite of the fact that peacekeeping is enjoying an unprecedented resurgence in the post–Cold War international system. Another reason is the parlous financial state of the OAU, arguably the poorest regional organization in the world. Many members have not paid their annual dues for several years. In 1995, for instance, members were in arrears of US$64 million, compared with an annual budget of just over $25 million. Finally, the marginalization of the continent has made it rather hard for the OAU to raise funds from the international community for conflict management purposes. . . . Put differently, the international community seems to be 'Africa fatigued'; that is, it is no longer willing to shoulder many of Africa's problems in the new world order. . . .

The lingering potency of the clause on non-interference [in the OAU Charter] remains a large constraint, since the majority of conflicts are within states. . . . At present, the OAU can only intervene in domestic situations that are not particularly sensitive, and even so, the host state still has the last say; that is, it has to give its stamp of approval before the OAU can get involved in its 'domestic affairs'. This limitation was recognized by Salim Ahmed Salim as early as 1991: 'questions of political participation are internal issues and there is therefore little room in such matters for innovation in conflict resolution, nor is there an explicit role for the OAU'. . . .

HALF-HEARTED EFFORTS

It is doubtful if African countries are sincere in their commitment to put an effective, indigenous conflict management organ in place in the continent. Their half-hearted financial commitment to the Peace Fund set up to finance the OAU's peacekeeping, peace-building and conflict-prevention activities bears that out. As late as 1995, members had contributed only $3.5 million to the fund. Predictably, much more money was realized from non-African sources: $5.2 million. But effective election monitoring and observer missions, which are not even as taxing as peacekeeping operations, require effective funding if they are to achieve the desired results. At the moment, the OAU is not in a position to shoulder such financial responsibility alone, given the poor state of the economies of a majority of its members and the reluctance of the international community to come to its aid. . . .

WHAT AFRICAN NATIONS MUST DO

African countries have to put in place a reliable multilateral conflict management mechanism, with or without external support, that can swiftly respond to conflicts anywhere in the continent in the future. Experience so far seems to show that reliance on external powers to resolve African conflicts is largely wishful thinking. The responses of the Great Powers to the humanitarian emergencies in Rwanda in 1994 and November 1996 confirm this pessimism. Apart from France and Canada, powers were reluctant to seize the initiative in a remote part of Africa, for fear of endangering the lives of their troops. It took the unexpected 'victory' of Zairean Tutsi rebels, and the 'voluntary' return of more than half a million refugees to Rwanda, to arrest the humanitarian tragedy.

Africa must design a conflict management mechanism that reflects its unique security predicament and needs in the future. A first step in that direction would be the identification of the continent's basic needs for an effective and self-reliant conflict management mechanism, under the auspices of the OAU. To be sure, the USA has suggested the setting up of a standing peacekeeping force for Africa. But it is doubtful if such a force will ever be formed, given the hostile attitude of Africans to an externally based intervention force. [South African president Nelson] Mandela, the most respected leader in Africa at the moment, would support such a force only if it were under OAU control. But it is doubtful whether the USA would finance and/or provide logistical support for a force over which it would have little or no control. What African scholars should do, then—and this is the area of research need—is to identify the existing capacity of the OAU in conflict management, the local resources available and the best and most efficient way of empowering Africa for effective and credible local conflict management roles.

Critical questions would have to be asked and answered. For instance, what are the types of capabilities needed for effective and timely intervention in African conflicts by Africans? What are the legal and institutional requirements for such a force? What capabilities does the OAU already have? How do we consolidate existing local capability, with or without external support? On what areas is local and external support to be targeted: peace strategies, for example? What types of assistance does the OAU need for effective intervention in conflict situations in Africa? Are they financial, training of future peacekeepers, logistics, information databases on conflicts and conflict situations, civilian personnel, intelligence gathering, communications equipment? How do we ensure that future peacekeeping operations are not taken over by external powers if they get involved in financing and equipping an African peacekeeping force? What is the most desirable relationship between the peace force, external powers and member states of the OAU? What will be the role or roles of officers in the OAU's Division of Conflict Management, Prevention and Resolution if a permanent peacekeeping force is put in place with or without external support? These are all important questions that must be answered comprehensively if we are to avoid the existing situation whereby Africa and the OAU slumber in the face of continental disorder, horrendous human suffering and humanitarian emergencies. That is perhaps the biggest challenge facing Africa and the rest of the world as we stand on the threshold of the next millennium.

> "Millions of men, women and children have withstood repression, . . . civil wars, border disputes and coups all in the name of nation-building."

ABOLISHING NATION-STATES CAN REDUCE CONFLICT

Ikaweba Bunting

In the following viewpoint, Ikaweba Bunting argues that the Western concept of the nation-state and the political borders drawn up by European powers in the nineteenth century have little utility for the everyday lives of Africans, yet constitute a source of continual political unrest. Attempts to develop nation-states in the image of industrialized foreign nations have resulted in repression, border disputes, civil wars, and ethnic conflict, he asserts. The Organization of African Unity erred in accepting the nation-state boundaries created by outsiders after African people successfully fought for independence from colonial rule. Africans must reject national borders that divide people in order to promote peaceful and equitable development, he concludes. Bunting is a regional communications officer for Oxfam, a relief, development, and advocacy organization dedicated to ending world poverty. He emigrated from the United States to Tanzania in 1974.

As you read, consider the following questions:

1. What personal experience involving the border between Tanzania and Kenya does Bunting describe?
2. Who controls what policies are undertaken by African states, according to the author?

Reprinted, with permission, from Ikaweba Bunting, "In Search of a New Africa," *The New Internationalist*, March 1996; ©1996 The New Internationalist.

On the way to Sinya there is a hill that you keep on your right as you head east. I call it the 'sacred hill of directions'. Past a small water-hole and an acacia tree and the hill shifts to your left until you reach a big Maasai *boma* (homestead). The route goes on from landmark to landmark until you finally reach the village. The open savannah is marked by cattle trails that disappear whenever a strong gust of wind stirs up the dust.

On this particular day a Tanzanian police officer who recognized me asked for a ride to the police post on the way. As we drove across the savannah we saw a herd of *swalla* (gazelles). My passenger asked me to turn the vehicle towards the animals so that he could hunt some. The police post is very remote and they often supplement their diet of maize and beans with game meat.

Which Side of the Border?

After driving around for some time with no success I decided that I must get on my way. It was then that I realized that I had forgotten to take note of any landmarks en route. I searched the horizon but could not see the hill I used for navigation. Being midday, it was also difficult to use the sun to figure out direction. I had a feeling that we were no longer in Tanzania but had crossed the border into Kenya. My companion, however, insisted that we were still in Tanzania.

As we drove zigzagging around, a young Maasai *moran* (warrior) appeared, striding across the plains with his spear over his shoulder. When we told him we were on our way to Sinya, he smiled and told us we had lost the way some distance. I asked him if we were in Kenya or Tanzania. He looked at me and then at my companion and asked: 'Why? Are you Kenyans or Tanzanians?' We replied: 'Tanzanian'. The young man then said with a laugh and a sidelong glance at the police officer: 'You are in Tanzania but you are lost!'

When we finally got back on track I located my sacred hill of directions. I was still convinced that we had been at least three kilometres inside Kenya. It eventually dawned on me that the young *moran* and the police officer had known all along where we were. But it made no difference to them which country we were in; whether we were on one side or the other of an imaginary line.

Nation-State Absurdities

This story illustrates the absurdities of the nation-state in Africa. Most of the time ordinary people simply ignore the borders. They cross them to go to market, to visit relatives and to work.

Occasionally a family's home is in one country and their farm-land in another.

The borders between countries are lines that were drawn on a map by the Europeans in order to establish the boundaries of their various colonial possessions. Most borders divided families or communities that shared the same socio-cultural history, spoke the same language and were often socio-political entities until they became subjects of different European monarchies. It is only by chance, by the legacy of the Berlin Conference of 1884, that we are called Tanzanians, Kenyans, Senegalese, Zimbabweans or Zambians.

In 1963 the Organization of African Unity (OAU) established nation-states based on colonial boundaries in its founding charter. This locked the new Africa into the task of building nations and national identities on a colonial foundation that by its very nature was inherently divisive and contradictory.

Then came the anti-colonial nationalism of the African liberation struggles of the 1950s and 1960s which was concerned with human rights, dignity and self-determination. The nationalist leaders were given a mandate—either by vote or by support for armed struggle and civil disobedience—to secure a situation that would restore cultural, social and economic freedom.

On those glorious nights at the midnight hour the various imperial representatives from Europe hauled down the flags of Britain, France or wherever, and presided over the raising of the flags of new African states. On those evenings football stadiums and meeting-grounds were filled beyond capacity with all the people waiting to experience the collective catharsis of uhuru (freedom).

AFTER INDEPENDENCE

During colonial rule the people and the leaders had struggled together as one. But once the ceremony was complete the leaders went with the colonial dignitaries to the Governor's mansion to celebrate. They drank champagne and danced to European music. Meanwhile, the masses remained in the stadium, drank local brew, played drums, and sang the songs and rhythms that they and their ancestors had sung for centuries.

Those nights were an omen, an early warning of what the future would become. On the one hand there were those people and organizations that advocated remaining part of the colonial empire with an élite sharing the privileges of their colonial masters, and on the other were militant nationalists who advocated sentiments of separation, self-determination and independence.

This dichotomy was not just confined to Africa; in the United States there was a growing social movement which also had two strands—a conservative integrationist philosophy and a Black Nationalist movement which expressed solidarity with African liberation struggles and anti-imperialist struggles throughout the world. Some black nationalists believed the solution to lie in a national homeland in the southern states of America; others proposed a return to Africa for part of the black population of America. Their objective was to build a pan-African movement which would be able to demand that the US and Europe respect the human and civil rights of black people.

ETHNIC DIVISIONS IN AFRICA

Source: Map reprinted, by permission, from *Why in the World? Adventures in Geography,* by George J. Demko, with Jerome Agel and Eugene Boe, produced by Jerome Agel. ©1992 by Jerome Agel. Published in trade paperback by Anchor Books/Doubleday.

The failure of the integrationists to become a successful part of mainstream America has spawned an adapted black nationalism which has sought to control local community economics, social services and politics without breaking from or revolting against capitalism and the dominant national power structure.

Losing Faith in Nationalism

I used to describe myself as a 'revolutionary pan-African Nationalist'. I thought that a strong socialist state was an absolute necessity for African freedom. Further, I believed that a union of those strong socialist states, a United States of Africa, was essential for the freedom and prosperity for all African peoples worldwide.

I no longer think the nation-state in Africa is viable—economically, politically or culturally.

My belief and hope that the post-colonial African nation could become a liberating institution for African people has been sobered by the reality of dependency. Today, finance and economic policy are controlled and managed directly by the World Bank and the International Monetary Fund (IMF). Political parties, governments and leaders in Africa solicit Western support in order to secure a power-base.

The international creditors control all the assets. The workers and peasants toil and sweat to service debts owed to the international bankers and multilateral agencies. So-called national budgets in many countries are more than 50-per-cent dependent on external financing. Development budgets are at least 90-per-cent dependent on donor funding. In other words, the African state is in receivership and cannot operate unless it gets money to do so from Western donors and financiers.

In Africa today only the symbols of sovereignty exist. There are flags, seats on the UN General Assembly, heads of state (sometimes more than one), armies, national currencies, ambassadors and Mercedes Benzes.

Developmentalism

The chain that imprisons African governments and consequently African people in this disempowering relationship is 'developmentalism'. Developmentalism is the ideology that believes the state is responsible for organizing society in such a way as to accelerate its progress into a free-market industrial society. This includes a parliament, a stock exchange, shopping malls, highways, automobile factories, pollution and increased crime. The idea of development is married to the idea of the nation-state. It is no wonder that the nation-state in Africa, having failed to replicate the Western socio-economic saga, is crumbling.

After 30 years I think African leaders, politicians, and business people, together with the international community, have a moral obligation to come to terms with the fundamental mistake that was made. Millions of men, women and children have withstood repression, torture, deprivation, suffering and death in uprisings, civil wars, border disputes and coups all in the name of nation-building and developing African states in the image and likeness of the industrialized Northern nations. It is too high a price to pay.

That said, does the failure and collapse of the nation-state (in Somalia, Liberia, Zaire and Rwanda) and the general failure of national development plans throughout the continent also mean the end of Pan-African nationalism?

PAN-AFRICANISM

I think not. I think there can still be a Pan-African unity—but of peoples not of states. This unity already exists in its potential form in the customs and cultures of the people, though the institutions and rulers of those nation-states keep the people divided and exploitable. Just as they were in colonial times.

Pan-Africanism is undergoing a resurgence in Africa, America, Latin America and Europe. Young people are exposed to popular culture that synthesizes African, African-American and Caribbean experiences. Many young Africans are travelling and experiencing racism in Europe and America. Emerging from these shared experiences and global communications is a global consciousness of African political and cultural solidarity that transcends the concept of the nation-state.

Transnational Pan-African solidarity is what can liberate Africa from the scourge and burden of perpetual 'Developing Nationhood'. The new Africa must be able to accommodate multiculturalism and the global reality of the twenty-first century. It must be able to create an environment that enables indigenous communities in villages and small towns to run their own affairs, control their own resources and benefit directly from the products of their own labour; and determine their own agenda for prosperity and peace.

Countries like Rwanda have a chance to lead the way, to do something different. That chance has been paid for in too much blood and suffering to be wasted in rebuilding the same structures that precipitated the implosion of the nation-state on its citizens in the first place.

FINDING OUR WAY

So what will rise out of the ashes of the post-colonial nation-state in Africa? For an answer let us emulate the attitude and adaptability of the young Maasai who gave me directions to Sinya. If you need to go someplace it doesn't matter what nation-state you claim as identity or which border there is to cross. The object of a journey is to get where you are going. The object of anti-imperialist nationalism and Pan-Africanism was not the nation-state but rather justice, equality, dignity, prosperity and freedom from domination.

We have lost the way and it is time to find our bearings, to relocate the 'sacred hill of directions' and get back on track. This would be the living tribute to those millions of African people who perished or are suffering in the name of nation-building and development.

"The *Africa Crisis Response Initiative (ACRI)* concept envisions a U.S. partnership with African . . . countries to build and improve African crisis response capabilities."

U.S. MILITARY ASSISTANCE TO AFRICAN ARMIES CAN IMPROVE PEACEKEEPING

Vincent D. Kern II

In September 1996 the United States proposed the creation of an African peacekeeping force, trained and equipped by the United States and other nations, that could intervene in conflicts and crisis situations where there was a threat of significant civilian casualties. Beginning in 1997, under a program called the Africa Crisis Response Initiative (ACRI), the United States provided training and equipment to military units of several African nations to help them carry out peacekeeping and humanitarian missions. In the following viewpoint, taken from 1997 testimony before Congress, Vincent D. Kern II argues that American training and support can teach African soldiers respect for civilian rule while enabling African nations to prevent a repetition of events such as the mass killings in Rwanda in 1994. Kern is deputy assistant secretary of defense for African affairs.

As you read, consider the following questions:

1. What does Kern emphasize as *not* being the goals of the Africa Crisis Response Initiative (ACRI)?
2. What training and equipment is the United States providing as part of the ACRI, according to the author?

Reprinted from Vincent D. Kern II's testimony before the House Committee on International Relations, Subcommittee on Africa, October 1, 1997.

D istinguished Members [of Congress], ladies and gentlemen, thank you for the opportunity today to appear before you and discuss what we at the Department of Defense view, as was stated by a member of the foreign press to one of my staff observing Africa Crisis Response Initiative (ACRI) training in Uganda, as "something positive for Africa." The concept of an ability to address humanitarian crises and peacekeeping requirements within Africa, by Africans, is not a new idea; our friends in Africa, our allies the British and the French, and several others have proposed this concept in several different forms in the past. The ACRI as we know it now originally began as a proposal to plan for the worst case scenario in central Africa, given the horrendous events in Rwanda in the Spring of 1994. We foresaw a military capability that would be able to rapidly assemble and deploy in order to prevent another descent into anarchy and the needless loss of life. We discussed this concept with both our African and non-African allies around the world. They recommended that we expand the concept beyond simply one region of Africa to that of something which could only address that problem, but also provide the capability to respond to future events. Therefore, the Department of Defense and the Department of State have further refined this concept to what is now known as the Africa Crisis Response Initiative, or the ACRI.

A TRAINING INITIATIVE

The ACRI concept envisions a U.S. partnership with African and non-African countries to build and improve African crisis response capabilities. It provides a unique opportunity to improve the operational capabilities of African militaries, making them better prepared to conduct either limited humanitarian or peacekeeping operations. Let me emphasize that the ACRI is a training initiative designed to create highly effective, rapid-deployable peacekeeping units, which can operate jointly. This expansion of the concept beyond that originally envisioned has generated a great deal of interest both within and outside Africa, and we will admit that there are those who are suspicious of our motives. We do not intend to create a standing African force and we are not providing training to create elite forces for instability. We are solely interested in providing training in those areas which are the traditional tasks associated with any peacekeeping operation: establishment of checkpoints, perimeter security, convoy security, the processing of displaced persons and the like. We are providing non-lethal equipment which is required by any organization anticipating involvement in peacekeeping operations or humanitarian crises. This includes communications gear, water purification units, some night vision binoculars, mine detectors, and the like. In order to ensure that individual soldiers have the necessary personal equipment, we have provided uniforms, boots, load-carrying equipment such as belts and packs, and entrenching tools. Just as for U.S. troops, force protection is of paramount importance to us. Therefore, we are providing ammunition for marksmanship training (and only for training) to enable peacekeepers to be able to properly defend themselves (as has been necessary in several recent peacekeeping operations). We have asked each of those nations volunteering troops for this initiative to sign end-use and non-transfer agreements to ensure that 1) this equipment is used only for peacekeeping and humanitarian purposes and 2) that it is ready if and when the call comes. We see these agreements as critical to the viability of the ACRI if it is ever called into action, and also contributing to our efforts to make this initiative as transparent as possible to the outside observer.

AFRICAN SOLUTIONS

A society cannot progress if it is being ripped apart by violence. And a region cannot integrate itself into the world community if nations within it are disrupting stability, generating refugees, deepening ethnic tensions, and illegally trafficking in arms.

The United States is sponsoring the Africa Crisis Response Initiative to enhance the capacity of African nations to prevent and contain disasters. This is part of a larger international effort and corresponds to the desire within the region to find African solutions to African problems.

Madeleine Albright, *U.S. Department of State Dispatch*, April 1998.

The training is provided by both the 3rd and 5th Special Forces Groups, both of whom have portions of the African continent within their areas of operations. The training lasts approximately 60 days, and is conducted by approximately 45 Special Forces trainers backed up by approximately 15 logistic, maintenance and support instructors. The training culminates in a Field Training Exercise (FTX), during which the unit's performance is evaluated. Those areas in which additional work is required are the subject of follow-up "sustainment" training which occurs at approximately four and eight months, respectively, following the completion of the first phase of training. The ACRI training is open to any and all nations who are interested in participating as either trainers or observers, given that the host nation approves their participation. We have actively sought to include both nongovernmental organizations and the media as not only observers, but also as role-playing participants in the training. In the training concluded in Uganda and Senegal, the participation of both those communities resulted in a greatly enhanced and realistic training evolution. We seek their participation in all our future training, for this not only provides a better training environment, but it also creates a better sense of understanding as to our motives. We hope to see both communities involved in the training in Malawi, and we invite their inquiries.

AN IMPORTANT OPPORTUNITY

In conclusion, we see the ACRI as an opportunity not only for Africans, but also for ourselves. While enhancing African peacekeeping capabilities, it also improves our opportunity to demonstrate to others the American soldier's respect for democratic civilian authority and his concern for human rights and individual dignity. We truly see the ACRI as "something positive for Africa."

> "The U.S. training gives the armed forces of developing nations significant new skills that have been used to repress dissent."

U.S. MILITARY ASSISTANCE TO AFRICAN ARMIES IS HARMFUL

Scott Nathanson

Scott Nathanson is a senior researcher for Demilitarization for Democracy, an organization that advocates reductions in the size of military establishments in developing nations. In the following viewpoint, he criticizes U.S. policy of providing training and equipment to the armed forces of African nations, such as that provided in 1997 through the Africa Crisis Response Initiative. African armies in too many cases have little regard for human rights and civilian rule, he asserts. Because of this, U.S. military assistance not only does little to prevent conflict, but can instead be used to help armies repress political dissent. Nathanson concludes that U.S. military aid should be withheld from nations under undemocratic regimes.

As you read, consider the following questions:

1. What examples of U.S. military aid to Africa does Nathanson describe?
2. What are the goals and wishes of human rights and democracy groups in Africa, according to the author?
3. In arguing against "constructive engagement" as a policy, what two African countries does Nathanson compare?

Reprinted from Scott Nathanson, "U.S. Should Stop Boosting Africa's Armies," Newsday, November 19, 1997, by permission of the author.

President Bill Clinton has just put the finishing touches on his "new" policy for Africa by appointing the Rev. Jesse Jackson special envoy for the promotion of democracy in Africa. But before Jackson can start, he must understand what exactly he is promoting.

During her 1997 African tour, Hillary Rodham Clinton complimented the transition of so many African nations toward democracy, and pledged that U.S. policy would be to support freedom and peace in Africa. However, if you scratch the surface, a starkly different picture emerges.

TRAINING FOR REPRESSION

The Clinton administration is violating the first commandment of pro-democracy groups in Africa—Thou shalt not provide assistance to the independent and often corrupt armed forces of our nations.

The statistics are striking. Of the more than 3,400 African officers trained in the U.S. International Military Education and Training program in 1991–1995, 69 percent were from nations under authoritarian rule. Eighty-one percent of those trainees were in nations whose armed forces wield substantial political and economic power independent of a civilian government. The U.S. training gives the armed forces of developing nations significant new skills that have been used to repress dissent.

Similar training is provided on the ground in Africa through the United States' joint combat exercise programs. Again, the statistics show the preponderance of U.S. combat training in Africa is with authoritarian regimes (55 percent) or armed forces independent of civilian control (71 percent).

A perfect example of the mindless expansion of these exercises is that the United States quickly began to engage in training the Rwandan military after the 1994 Tutsi takeover. U.S. officials admit that some of these U.S.-trained troops may have "inadvertently" been used in Laurent Kabila's [successful 1997] rebellion in Zaire, now Congo. This is the same Kabila who is rejecting the pleas from the United States to allow human rights investigators into areas under his control.

THE AFRICA CRISIS RESPONSE INITIATIVE

On top of everything, a new Africa Crisis Response Initiative has been established that would accept only nations that "have military establishments that accept the supremacy of democratic civilian government," according to a July 7, 1997, State Department paper on the program. U.S special forces are training African troops that could respond to a crisis that threatened the stability of a nation or region, like the Rwandan genocide of 1994.

However, according to John Christiansen, the Crisis Response deputy coordinator, "minimum military efficiency" is now the entry standard instead of civilian rule. Only one of the seven nations slated to be trained can be qualified as a democracy. The fears of misuse of Crisis Response-equipped aid trained troops came true almost immediately, as the first troops trained under the program in Uganda were immediately sent to use their new skills in a counter-insurgency war against rebel forces.

Charlie Snyder, the deputy head of the Africa Bureau at the State Department, defended the continued involvement with

U.S. MILITARY ASSISTANCE FISCAL YEAR 1997

($ in thousands)

African nation recipient	Foreign Military Sales (FMS) contracts	Commercial Sales (CS) licenses	Excess Defense Articles (EDA) grants	International Military Education and Training (IMET) grants
Algeria	0	57,938	0	61
Angola	0	11,618	0	174
Botswana	439	3,013	755	391
Eritrea	2,478	900	0	413
Ethiopia	1,508	0	0	313
Ghana	0	4,383	0	243
Kenya	779	617	0	304
Mali	0	1	0	152
Morocco	6,942	15,798	90,886	812
Senegal	1,965	0	0	697
South Africa	154	10,865	0	656
Tanzania	0	597	0	5
Tunisia	15,235	2,038	12,452	837
Uganda	3,872	4	0	342
Zambia	0	808	0	172
Zimbabwe	91	122	0	298

Sources: Department of State, Congressional Presentation for Foreign Operations, Fiscal Year 1999 (Washington, DC: Department of State, 1998), pp. 1011 and 1146; Congressional Record, 4 March 1998, p. E2956; and Arms Sales Monitoring Project, Federation of American Scientists, Arms Sales Monitor No. 36 (28 February 1998), p. 5. Daniel Volman, "The Development of the Africa Crisis Response Initiative," an African Policy Report, April 23, 1998.

dictators on the African continent at a panel discussion. What did he call this policy? "Constructive engagement."

Ironically, this is the same term the Reagan administration used to justify its continued engagement with the apartheid South African government in the 1980s.

The use of the term "constructive engagement" shows the Clinton administration's myopia toward Africa. Officials continue to claim that the only way to get abusive armed forces to make the transition to democracy is to train them to be more effective militaries. There is scant evidence to back this up. Somalia, Rwanda, Zaire? Which one of these nations has armed forces more respectful of civilian rule and human rights because of our "constructive engagement?"

REMOVE THE MILITARY FROM POLITICS

If Jackson truly wants to help promote democracy in Africa, then he should begin by speaking to the leaders of the organizations fighting for democracy and human rights in their nations. These people will tell him that the military must be removed from the political process. Military and government officials must be held accountable for their abuses of power. The press must be free. Women must be given increased access to political participation. Economic opportunity must be increased in both urban and rural areas so everyone feels the benefit of democracy. In all, we must understand that democracy in Africa should be supported by, not imported from, the United States.

A "new" policy for Africa is possible if our government looks to promote the good of the people of that continent, not its leaders. A code of conduct on military assistance . . . that would prohibit any U.S. assistance to governments that are undemocratic [and] abuse the human rights of their people would be an excellent start.

This is the kind of engagement that would be truly constructive, not only for Africans, but for Americans as well. The end of constructive engagement in South Africa brought a new strategic, economic, and political partner for America. Continued constructive engagement in Rwanda has brought more strife, instability and suffering to the nations in the Great Lakes region of Africa.

Which one would you say worked better?

"This is a situation where achieving justice at the level of individual cases is less important than putting a stop to the endless cycle of violence."

WAR-CRIMES TRIBUNALS MIGHT PROLONG VIOLENCE IN RWANDA

Leo J. DeSouza

The central African nation of Rwanda is divided between the Hutu and Tutsi ethnic groups. In April 1994 the Hutu-dominated Rwandan government and military instigated an organized campaign to kill Tutsis; an estimated 800,000 were slain before Tutsi-led rebels overthrew the government in July 1994. The international community has since condemned the actions of the Hutus as genocide; both the new Tutsi-led government and a special tribunal of the United Nations have acted to investigate and punish those responsible. In the following viewpoint, Leo J. DeSouza argues the world community must take into account that history of Hutu-Tutsi relations, including past Tutsi atrocities committed against the Hutus. Trying to punish all individuals who participated in the 1994 genocide would prolong conflict in Rwanda, he argues. To ensure future peace, a full investigation of the 1994 events must be coupled with a general amnesty for all but high-ranking officials. DeSouza, a former orthopedic surgeon consultant in Uganda, moved to the United States in 1971 and practices medicine in Minneapolis, Minnesota.

As you read, consider the following questions:

1. What are the historical roots of Hutu-Tutsi antagonism, according to DeSouza?
2. What is the current situation of Hutu prisoners in Rwanda, according to the author?

Reprinted from Leo J. DeSouza, "Assigning Blame in Rwanda," *The Washington Monthly*, September 1997, with permission from *The Washington Monthly*, 1611 Connecticut Ave. NW, Washington, DC 20009; 202-462-0128.

On September 26, 1996, the United Nations's International Criminal Tribunal for Rwanda began genocide trials in Arusha, a small town at the foot of Mt. Kilimanjaro in Tanzania. The man in the dock was Jean-Paul Akayesu, former mayor of Taba in Rwanda and the first Hutu to be tried by the Tribunal. He is accused of atrocities in his district, where 2,000 Tutsi lie buried in two mass graves after being hacked to death with machetes.

Akayesu pleaded not guilty and asked for postponement, but when the trial resumed in January of 1997, the international community renewed its cry for justice, i.e., for the blood of the Hutu.

THE TRAGIC EVENTS OF 1994

Certainly, the public outrage is understandable. The story of the majority Hutu population's massacre of Rwanda's Tutsi minority is one of unimaginable viciousness and violence. The events immediately preceding the massacre and the subsequent months prior to the overthrow of the government by Tutsi rebels are familiar to—and abhorred by—most readers: On April 6, 1994, Rwandan President Juvénal Habyarimana was returning from a peace conference in Tanzania. Also aboard his plane was Cyprien Ntaryamira, president of neighboring Burundi. Both were members of the region's majority Hutu tribe. Preparing to land on the palace grounds, the plane was shot down, killing both men.

Reaction was instantaneous. Within hours the Rwandan Presidential Guard (dominated by Hutu) went on a rampage, killing Rwanda's Tutsi Prime Minister and other members of the opposition party sympathetic to the Tutsi. Soldiers and militiamen joined in. They fanned out across the city looking for Tutsi.

The slaughter had begun.

From Kigali the killing spread to towns, prefectural capitals, and hillside settlements. Across the country, the Tutsi were massacred in their homes, in open fields, along broad roads, and even as they hid in the bushes. They were slain with stones and axes, machetes and clubs, hand grenades and guns.

In a Roman Catholic church, an orange brick building in the town square of one village, 1,200 Tutsi sought refuge. The local Hutu mayor had promised police protection. But the following morning, soldiers appeared, blew open the locked church door with a hand grenade, and fired into the huddled mass. They returned the next morning to finish off those who had survived, leaving only bodies, blood and silence.

In another "safe" church, a Hutu mob swarmed in, hacking and clubbing frightened women and children to death. Tutsi patients disappeared from hospitals; Tutsi students from schools.

Tutsi teenage girls were raped. Hutu mothers with babies strapped to their backs killed Tutsi mothers with babies strapped to their backs; Hutu 10-year-olds killed Tutsi 10-year-olds. Before it was over, half a million Rwandans were dead. They were almost all Tutsi, along with a few Hutu who had refused to go along with the carnage.

As the Tutsi were being decimated in Rwanda, Tutsi exiles living in Uganda felt the time for action was at hand. Calling themselves the "Rwandan Patriotic Front," the rebels entered the country from the north and advanced swiftly toward the capital. They had had a running battle with the Hutu ever since the country gained independence in 1962 and democratic elections had put the more numerous Hutu in power. Now, pushing with the ferocity of the dispossessed, the exiled Tutsi overran the country and by July 18 had taken over the capital and declared victory.

LURIE'S WORLD

Lurie's World ©1996 Worldwide Copyright by CARTOONEWS INTERNATIONAL Syndicate, N.Y.C., USA. Used with permission.

The victorious Tutsi quickly ascertained that the violence that had seized the country since the president's plane crash was not the result of random acts. They determined that the killings had been organized, encouraged, even ordered by the Hutu government officials at the highest level, whose intent had been to wipe out the Tutsi from Rwanda. Within two weeks, the Tutsi government announced that they would "proceed with war-crimes trials of . . . the ousted government and . . . civilians suspected of taking part in the genocidal attacks." The following December, the UN created the International War-Crimes Tribunal for Rwanda, with trials to be held in the neutral territory of Tanzania. Some 400 Hutu were to be charged with planning and organizing the massacres.

To those following the conflict on the evening news, the Hutu-Tutsi conflict seems entirely straightforward, if somewhat incredible. Comparisons to the Nazi extermination of the Jews have been tossed around. But the Rwanda conflict, while tragic, is considerably more complicated. The Tutsi of Central Africa are not quite the peace-loving victims of Western imagination. Over the years, they have committed a long list of atrocities of their own. The international community's ignorance of this history has caused them to treat the Tutsi who now rule Rwanda as noble victims—and to ignore the danger that the Tutsi will use their newfound power to exact bloody revenge on the Hutu. And if that happens, the cycle of genocidal violence in Rwanda will only continue. (Already, in eastern Congo Tutsi are believed to be exterminating the fleeing Hutu refugees.) The only hope of ending that cycle lies in understanding the full history of Hutu-Tutsi relations and adopting an approach which takes that history into account.

A Centuries-Old Grudge

The Hutu's fear and hatred of the Tutsi has its roots in centuries of abuse. The Hutu were in Rwanda long before anyone, other than the Bantu tribes. The Tutsi arrived much later, around the 15th century, from the northeast. Theirs was a slow and peaceful infiltration. But over time they used their cattle and their warring skills to build their power and prestige. Whenever the Hutu needed the use of cattle, they worked for the Tutsi owner as payment. This simple arrangement eventually crystallized into a feudal-type class system. Land, cattle, and power were consolidated in the hands of the Tutsi, and the Hutu became serfs. Hutu peasants bound themselves to individual Tutsi lords, giving land, produce, and personal services in exchange for the lord's protection and use of his cattle. Tall and aristocratic in bearing, the Tutsi claimed they were divinely ordained to rule. In this manner, the Tutsi minority—between 10 and 20 percent of the population—held dominion over the Hutu for 400 years.

In 1885 Europe's colonial powers convened at a conference in Berlin to carve up the African continent. Rwanda was pronounced a German colony. The Germans ruled Rwanda through the Tutsi king, or Mwami, who, in turn, used German forces to strengthen his own position. Since the Europeans governed their colonies ostensibly to enlighten poor backward souls and to introduce them to the concept of fairness, one would have thought that the Europeans would have attempted to relieve the Hutu from serfdom. Far from it. What little flexibility had previously existed between the Tutsi lords and the Hutu vanished during the colonial era. It was during this period that the Mwami came closer to absolute rule than at any other time. Hutu rebellion was dealt with swiftly: Villages were burnt and leaders executed—with guns supplied by Europeans. It was no different when the Belgians took over during World War I. From 1916 until Rwandan independence in 1962, the Belgians ruled through the Tutsi aristocracy.

The Europeans were always attracted to the Tutsi. Unlike the Hutu, who are a dark people, short and squat, with coarse features, the Tutsi are tall and fair, with finer features that reminded Europeans of themselves. The Germans and Belgians romanticized the tall Tutsi as Africa's elite. Schools were open to them and admission to college was fixed in their favor, by requiring applicants to pass a minimum height test. They were assured of the best jobs.

This modus operandi was not unusual among colonial rulers. They often selected an elite minority group to help administer their far-flung colonies. It was a way of creating a client community, a tactic that divided the colonized population while consolidating colonial rule. In Lebanon, the Maronites were the anointed ones; in Egypt, the Copts; and in northern India, the Sikhs. In Rwanda, the system was even more flagrant: It consolidated the higher status of the Tutsi by emphasizing the differences between them and the Hutu. The Belgians even introduced identity cards, requiring everyone to be recognized by their tribe.

ESCALATING VIOLENCE

In the years leading up to Rwanda's independence, the country's High Council, a Tutsi body, called for urgent training of the Tutsi elite in preparation for self-government—a plain attempt to perpetuate Tutsi dominance. The Hutu leaders countered with "The Manifesto of the Bahutu" which sought to end the Tutsi's stranglehold on the government. The Belgians ignored the manifesto; the Tutsi spurned it. One Tutsi group said: "Relations between us and them have forever been based on servitude; therefore, there is no feeling of fraternity whatsoever between them and us. . . . Since our Kings have conquered all of the Hutu's lands by killing their monarchs and enslaving their people, how can they now pretend to be our brothers?" Tensions mounted in 1959. In a last ditch attempt to hold onto power, the Tutsi began massacring any Hutu they believed might stand in their way. Francois Karera, a senior politician in the former Hutu government, now an exile in eastern Congo, was a young teacher in 1959 when the Hutu rose up for the first time. He recalls that period as one when he, as an educated Hutu, was "hunted" by Tutsi for daring to aspire to a higher standing than a mere peasant farmer. But the Hutu prevailed. In the sporadic violence of that period, more than 20,000 Tutsi were displaced. In 1962, Rwanda became independent and held national elections. The Hutu candidate Kayibanda was elected President following a Hutu victory at the polls.

This did not sit well with the Tutsi. Their militants organized into guerrilla bands, and casualties escalated. Between 1961 and 1966, the Inyenzi, or cockroaches, as the Tutsi militants called themselves, launched 10 major attacks from neighboring countries—Uganda, Tanzania, Burundi, and Zaire. The rebellions prompted severe retaliation from the Hutu in power. In 1963, about 10,000 Tutsi were killed following an Inyenzi attack from Burundi. Eventually defeated, they fell back into exile. Tutsi refugees totaled 150,000. The story repeated itself in 1973 when more Tutsi were killed on suspicion of their involvement in a coup in which the Hutu General Habyarimana deposed Rwanda's first President. (Habyarimana subsequently died in the fateful 1994 plane crash that triggered the latest round of violence.)

Events in neighboring Burundi served to further inflame the Hutu-Tutsi hatreds in Rwanda. Rwanda and Burundi are practically replicas of one another. Alike in size and population, they have the same tribal mix of Hutu and Tutsi, share much of the same history, and were part of the same colony.

Like Rwanda, Burundi became independent in 1962. But unlike Rwanda, Burundi's Tutsi minority has retained power and, to this day, rules the country. In the late '60s and early '70s, when the Tutsi in Burundi began to fear that the country's more numerous Hutu would come to power as they had in Rwanda, the Tutsi came up with a simple solution: eliminate the Hutu in Burundi. In 1972, they set out to massacre every Hutu with an education, a government job, or money. Within three months 250,000 Hutu were dead, their homes destroyed.

"Many Hutu were taken from their homes at night," wrote David Lamb of the Los Angeles Times in his book The Africans. "Others received summonses to report to the police station. So obedient, subservient, and hopeless had the Hutus become that they answered the summons, which even the most unlearned soul knew was really an execution notice. Sometimes, when the death quotas at the prisons and police stations had been filled for the day, the queued-up Hutu were told to return the next day. They dutifully complied. The few Hutu who tried to escape the executioners seemed to make only token attempts. It was a pathetic sight. They would walk down the main road toward the border. If the Tutsi gendarme stopped them," he continued, "they would turn quietly back."

A quarter of a million Hutu were slain in three months, but the world did not take notice. Nobody called it genocide, then or now. And nobody asked that the Tutsi in Burundi be tried. (To this day, sporadic killing of the Hutu continues in Burundi, and recently there has been an ominous escalation.)

WHAT NEXT?

Meanwhile, for lack of funds and assistance, Rwanda's unsuccessful Tutsi rebels lived quietly in exile until October of 1990. At that time, using Uganda as a base, the Rwandan Patriotic Front launched an invasion. Their stated aim: to take over the government in order to protect the Tutsi. By then, they had regrouped, retrained, and rearmed with new and heavier weapons. The initial assault was repelled by the Hutu government, but skirmishes continued through 1991 and 1992. A cease-fire was called in January 1993, but the Tutsi attacked again. On August 4, 1993, a peace agreement was signed in Tanzania. Implementation of the agreement, however, was slow. And when Rwanda's Hutu President was killed in April of 1994, there was widespread fear among the Hutu that another Tutsi rebellion was again underway. "In the Hutu mind, the Tutsi were going to bring back their regime; we the Hutu were going to work for them again, and the educated Hutu would be killed as in 1959," says Francois Karera, who insists the Hutu's subsequent massacre of the Tutsi was driven by fear and self-preservation. "The Hutu were determined," claims Karera, "not to allow the Tutsi to repeat history."

In contrast to the indifference with which the international community greeted the 1972 massacre of Hutu in Burundi, the 1994 massacre of Tutsi in Rwanda provoked global outrage. Television photographers and newspaper reporters told the tragedy as it unfolded, without reference to events in Burundi or what had previously transpired in Rwanda. The whole world judged the Hutu crimes as an isolated act.

Now that they are back in power, the Tutsi of Rwanda have embarked on their own broad investigation and prosecution of Hutu *genocidaires*. In contrast to the international tribunal in Tanzania, which is focused on the leaders of the massacre, the Rwandan government's probe is centered on lower level civilians. Early reports are troubling. In the first week of the new year, a Rwandan court at Kibungo sentenced two Hutu men to death after a four-hour trial. More trials have now begun in Kigali and Byumba. The prisons in Rwanda are currently packed with 85,000 Hutu. A facility built to hold 500 inmates now holds 7,000. Prisoners cannot sit or lie down for lack of space. So they stand, four to a square yard, in the muddy central courtyard. It takes hours to reach the latrines or the cooking fires. For 7,000 people there are 21 latrines, 5 of them designated for dysentery sufferers who try to stay nearby. There is no protection against heavy rain and many prisoners' feet show signs of rotting from gangrene. A few die every day. "It is horrific," said Dr. Alison Davis, of the relief agency Doctors Without Borders. "They are being treated like animals. It is true that some or many may have been involved in the killing, but the way they are treated is not justice."

A GENERAL AMNESTY

Whatever their motivation—fear or simple hatred—the Hutu should, of course, be held accountable for their slaughter of the Tutsi. But while it's advisable to punish the Hutu leaders who incited the population to commit the atrocities, it is a grave mistake to go after the low level perpetrators. True, many crimes would go unpunished. But this is a situation where achieving justice at the level of individual cases is less important than putting a stop to the endless cycle of violence. If, with the acquiescence of the international community, the Tutsi government continues to prosecute low-level Hutus without also holding local Tutsis responsible for their past deeds, the Hutu of Rwanda will feel justified in taking their counter-revenge the next time they're on top. The only way to end the bloodletting in Rwanda once and for all is to declare a general amnesty for all but the highest level perpetrators and establish a truth commission similar to the one in South Africa, charged with investigating the fate of victims on both sides even as it forgives most of their attackers. This could initially be conducted under the aegis of the Organization of African Unity, or the UN, or both. But unless it is done, another genocide is waiting to happen: The Tutsi will kill the Hutu, and then, of course, the Hutu will kill the Tutsi.

> "Only the assurance of world order can ensure that genocide is not repeated."

WAR-CRIMES TRIBUNALS MUST PUNISH THOSE RESPONSIBLE FOR GENOCIDE IN RWANDA

Alain Destexhe

Alain Destexhe is president of the International Crisis Group, a private organization. As director of Medicins sans Frontieries International (Doctors Without Borders) from 1991 to 1995, he was directly involved in relief operations in Rwanda in 1994. Destexhe later became a senator in Belgium's parliament and initiated an official Belgian government inquiry into the Rwandan genocide. In the following viewpoint, excerpted from his book *Rwanda and Genocide in the Twentieth Century*, Destexhe argues that the actions of the Rwandan Armed Forces (FAR) and Rwandan government in 1994 are directly comparable to Nazi Germany's genocide against Jews during World War II. Perpetrators of the genocidal actions in Rwanda must be condemned and punished by the global community to enact justice and to prevent the repetition of such tragedies.

As you read, consider the following questions:

1. What actions did the Rwandan government take to pave the way for its 1994 killings according to Destexhe?
2. What three reasons exist to bring the perpetrators of genocide to trial, in the author's view?
3. According to the author, what four categories of responsibility for genocide can be identified?

The discovery of the Nazi concentration camps at the end of the Second World War may have aroused shock and horror throughout the world and raised the popular cry, 'Never again!' but other voices were less certain that this particular lesson of history had really been learned. The Italian writer, Primo Levi, who himself survived Auschwitz, rejected the idea that the camps could be explained away either as an accident of history or an expression of mid-twentieth century barbarism. He saw the risk that they could well serve as an exemplary model for to-day's world: 'The simple fact is that it has happened once, and it could all happen again.'. . .

It took exactly 50 years for Primo Levi's prediction that 'it could all happen again' to be realised. Even if the circumstances of the Jewish genocide are different in regard both to the scale of the killings and in the methods used, it or something very like it has indeed happened again. Although it is true that previous massacres of Hutus in Burundi and Tutsis in Burundi and Rwanda seemed very like acts of genocide, they were never part of a concerted plan aimed at what might be called a Final Solution to the Tutsis 'problem' in Rwanda (although there are instinctive reservations about making this kind of comparison).

RACIST IDEOLOGY

Just as Hitler's grand plan was founded on an engrained European anti-semitism which he played on by singling out the Jews as the source of all Germany's ills, the Hutu radicals are inheritors of the colonial lunacy of classifying and grading different ethnic groups in a racial hierarchy. While the Jews were described by the Nazis as 'vermin', the Tutsis were called *invenzi* ('the cockroaches that have to be crushed'). Anti-Tutsi propaganda presented them as a 'minority, well-off and foreign'—so similar to the image developed to stigmatise the Jews—and thus an ideal scapegoat for all Rwanda's problems. The radicalisation of the Hutu began around 1990, when their monopoly of power was first seriously challenged by the army of the [Tutsi-led] Rwandan Patriotic Front (RPF). This was reinforced by the power-sharing conditions of the 1993 Arusha Accords which offered credible possibilities for national reconciliation and peace for the majority of Rwandans at the expense of the ruling Hutu parties. At that point, the Hutu extremists decided on the relentless pursuit of Tutsis and moderate Hutus.

The plot was devised within the close circle surrounding President Juvénal Habyarimana. From 1990, at the instigation, and with the active complicity of Habyarimana and his government, massacres of Tutsis increased and went unpunished. Two Hutu parties—a wing of the Movement Républican National for Development (MRND), 'the only party to have held power since independence, and the Coalition for the Defence of the Republic (CDR), a more recently created, extremist group—increasingly promoted a racist ideology. With the complicity of the army and those in power, they developed a simple strategy for retaining control through the formation of militias and the manipulation of the media, both of which later became tools of the genocide itself.

The militias were set up in order to spread terror. The *Interhamwe* ('those who attack together') and the *Impuzamugambi* ('those who only have one aim'), the youth wings of the MRND and CDR respectively, soon claimed 50,000 members between them. They carried out intimidation raids and 'punitive expeditions' against the terrorized Tutsi population as well as Hutus who supported democracy and negotiations with the RPF. It is not as well-known as it should be that for the previous two or three years an impressive movement in favour of a multi-party system, the rule of law and a respect for human rights had grown up in Rwanda. There were a large number of individual initiatives, the monopoly of one-party power had been broached and independent human rights organisations set up. In the eyes of the CDR and MRND these democrats were traitors who only merited the fate of all traitors. Although there were certainly many obstacles, political change seemed inevitable and reconciliation hovered on the horizon, but only at the expense of the racist parties who had the most to lose from them—and everything to gain by preventing them.

WARNING SIGNS

Between 1991 and 1994, alarm bells were ringing and signs were there to be read, in the form of massacres that went unpunished. These warning signals were even reported by the UN Human Rights Commission. In 1993 and 1994, thousands of militia members were given arms and military training by the Rwandan Armed Forces (the FAR) which, thanks to French generosity, grew from 5000 to 40,000 men, thus enabling it to take on both the RPF and the internal opposition. In September 1992, a document originating from FAR headquarters established the distinction between the principal enemy and their supporters. The first is defined as:

> Tutsis inside the country or outside, extremists and longing to return to power, who have never recognised and never will recognise the reality of the 1959 social revolution [when the Tutsi

were thrown out of power], and who would take back power in Rwanda by any means possible, including the use of arms.

The second is described as: 'anybody who gives any kind of support to the main enemy' (the Hutu opposition).

In a country which receives virtually no information from the outside world, local media, particularly the radio, play an essential role. For a large part of the population, a transistor radio is the only source of information and therefore has the potential for exerting a powerful influence. Rwandan radio broadcasts are in two languages, French and the national language, Kinyarwanda, which is spoken by all Rwandans. Less than a year before the genocide began, two close associates of President Habyarimana (his brother-in-law Alphonse Ntimavunda and Félicien Kabuga, a businessman married to his daughter) set up the 'private' radio station, popularly known as Radio Mille Collines. Assured of a large audience thanks to regular programmes of popular music, the programmes in Kinyarwanda broadcast unceasing messages of hate, such as 'the grave is only half full. Who will help us to fill it?'. Christened 'the radio that kills' by its opponents, it was the basic instrument of propaganda for the Hutu extremists, and the militias rallied in support of its slogans.

The monthly journal *Kangura* also contributed to spreading anti-Tutsi racism. Two months after war broke out in October 1990, it published a 'Call to the Conscience of the Bahutu Peoples' accompanied by the 'Ten Bahutu Commandments'. The eighth of these ten commandments pronounced, 'The Hutus should stop feeling any pity for the Tutsis', and the tenth ordered, 'regard as a traitor every Hutu who has persecuted his brother Hutu for reading, spreading and teaching this [Hutu] ideology'. Intent on bringing the ethnic question into the political process, the journal called for all available means to be used to prevent a successful conclusion to the negotiations with the RPF. For the racist Hutu parties, the President had betrayed his people by signing the Arusha Accords, which he had been obliged to accept as a result of international pressure.

THE GENOCIDE BEGINS

On 6 April 1994, the plane carrying President Habyarimana and President Cyprien Ntariyamira of Burundi was shot down by rocket-fire. Although it is not yet known who was behind this assassination, it is clear that it acted as the fuse for the eruption of the violence which led to the greatest tragedy in the history of the country. Even before the national radio station announced the death of the President, death lists were being circulated to facilitate the identification of Hutu opponents, mostly those who supported the democratic movement or promoted human rights. Several ministers in the transition government were assassinated, including members of the democratic opposition such as Prime Minister Agathe Uwilingiyima. These extensive killings veiled the essential fact that although Hutu intellectuals and opponents were being killed, the intention was to systematically eliminate every single Tutsi. As this fundamental distinction was not immediately obvious, neither was it clear at the beginning that a genocide was underway, especially in the growing confusion caused by a new RPF attack.

THERE MUST BE JUSTICE

Rwanda has begun to deal with the 90,000 suspected killers who overflow its jails. "Of course everyone who murdered should be punished, but are you going to execute 90,000 people?" asks Jane Rasmussen, a human rights lawyer. Rwandan officials estimate that some 2,000 people—leaders, wholesale killers, and torturers—will be shot. Many others presumably will receive prison terms. Some of the accused planners of the genocide are being tried by a UN tribunal in Tanzania.

None of this goes easily. Rwanda lacks experienced judges and prosecutors, and the UN tribunal has been plagued by bureaucratic mismanagement. Some murder witnesses have been killed before they could testify.

Nevertheless, as Rasmussen says, "Before the region can be stable, there must be justice." It will not solve all the many problems: poverty, crowding, displaced masses, political instability. But it would be a start; it might even deter more massacres. And for now, justice is about the most that can be hoped for.

Mike Edwards, *National Geographic*, June 1997.

As the stereotypes of physical characteristics do not always provide sufficient identification—and can even be totally misleading—it was the identity cards demanded at the roadblocks set up by the militias that acted as the signature on a death warrant for the Tutsis. As control of the road could not alone ensure that no Tutsi escaped, the militia leaders divided up the territory under their control so that one man was allocated for every ten households in order to systematically search for Tutsis in their immediate localities. In this way every Tutsi family could be denounced by somebody who knew the members personally: pupils were killed by their teachers, shop owners by their customers, neighbour killed neighbour and husbands killed wives in order to save them from a more terrible death. Churches where Tutsis sought sanctuary were particular targets and the scene of some of the worst massacres: 2800 people in Kibungo, 6000 in Cyahinda, 4000 in Kibeho, to give just a few examples. In Rwanda, the children of mixed marriages take the ethnic group of the father and, although many of the Hutu killers—including some militia leaders—had Tutsi mothers, so effective was the indoctrination programme, that even this apparently counted for nothing. Radio Mille Collines encouraged the violence with statements such as that made at the end of April 1994, 'By 5 May, the country must be completely cleansed of Tutsis.' Even the children were targeted: 'We will not repeat the mistake of 1959. The children must be killed too.' The media directly influenced Hutu peasants, convincing them that they were under threat and encouraging them to 'make the Tutsis smaller' by decapitating them. In the northern areas occupied by the RPF, the peasants were astonished that the Tutsi soldiers did not have horns, tails and eyes that shone in the dark as they had been described in radio programmes.

WORLD PRESS MISSES THE STORY

The genocide spread rapidly to cover the whole country under the control of the government army. By the end of April, it was estimated that 100,000 people had been killed. Africa had never known massacres on such a scale, yet the world was blind to the reality of events. Reviewing headlines in the French and English language press in those first weeks, there is a clear attempt to present the massacres as part of a civil war: 'Rwanda on Fire', 'Fierce Clashes', 'Slaughter', 'Massacre', 'Civil War', 'Bloody Horror', 'Rwanda Anarchy', 'Fall of Kigali Imminent'. It is rare to find a newspaper that made a distinction between the assassinations of specifically targeted Hutus and the systematic elimination of all Tutsis. It took three weeks from 6 April—a long time in the world of CNN-style news—before editorials finally began comparing the situation in Rwanda with Germany under Nazism and referring to it as a genocide. Overall, however, the word genocide rarely appeared in the main headlines—certainly not often enough to raise the awareness of the general public to the extraordinary event that was taking place. . . .

JUSTICE MUST BE DONE

The perpetrators of genocide should permanently lose any legitimacy as rulers of their people. They should be outlawed by the international community and brought to trial for their crimes. In the case of Rwanda, no attempt should be made to negotiate with those responsible for the genocide of the Tutsis: they are not only directly responsible for this worst possible crime against humanity but also for the exodus from Rwanda and the catastrophic events in Goma which followed. When the Allied forces won victory in 1945, there was never any question of providing a role for the Nazi party in the new Germany, nor of considering just how small a fraction of the population it really represented. The Nazis were banned outright and the authors of genocide then, as should happen in Rwanda today, lost any right to participate in public life. . . .

There is an urgent need for national reconciliation in Rwanda, but this must not be at the expense of justice, otherwise the opposite effect will be produced and the murderers reinstated. In Germany, at the end of the war, the Nazis and the democrats did not sit down together to discuss reconciliation. Likewise the international community should now give its support exclusively to the new, mainly RPF, government which is the legitimate government of Rwanda today. Its legitimacy does not come from the ballot box, but from its victory over a racist regime and its stated intention of working towards national reconciliation between the different groups and parties. But at the beginning of 1995, it seemed that the worst possible scenario was being realised with the FAR rallying huge numbers of refugees to take up the combat once again and 'finish off the job'. The slogan 'the Tutsis took 25 years to return with 200,000 refugees but we will only need a few weeks with two million to draw on' has been widely heard. Renewal of the conflict will simply lead the international community once again to justify its reasons for not getting involved: the (new) civil war, the RPF minority in the face of the 'reality of the Hutu majority'. And the genocide will be lost sight of, consigned to the history books.

CRIME AND PUNISHMENT

The lack of a global commitment for dealing with a crime of this scale represents not only a moral defeat on the part of the international community, but also a grave political error. Those who bear the greatest responsibility for the genocide must be brought to trial for three reasons.

First, of course, for the the sake of the victims. The renaissance philosopher, Hugo Grotius, stated that punishment is necessary to defend the honour of the injured party who would otherwise be degraded if no punishment were accorded to his aggressor.

Second, if a killer is pursued under criminal law by a state because he has broken the laws of that state and community, not simply because he has deprived a family of one of its members, then the authors of a genocide should be pursued not only because they have killed hundreds of thousands of people, but, even more so, because they have violated the moral order of the human race by attempting to destroy one of its member parts. There is no future for humanity if one, cohesive, part of it risks extermination by another whose members will never be punished. . . .

The third and final reason is the political imperative that those responsible for the genocide in Rwanda should be punished. If this does not happen, the whole world, but particularly Africa, risks being caught up in a spiral of violence and there is enormous potential for further ethnic cleansing and genocide. Only the assurance of world order can ensure that genocide is not repeated. . . .

Trials must be held, not only for the victims themselves, but even more so for the moral order throughout international society, which is under grave threat if further abominations of a similar kind are encouraged through a lack of resolve and political will.

CATEGORIES OF RESPONSIBILITY

Four categories of responsibility can be identified:

1. Those who instigate the plot. Genocide does not happen by chance nor out of spontaneous collective madness and in Rwanda, the plan was conceived by a small core of people close to President Habyarimana. It was they who drew up the blueprints for the militias, death squads and Radio Mille Collines, even if they were not the ones to transform them into a reality: they made sure that there was no blood on their hands. Nevertheless, there is no question that these are the most guilty and must be made to stand trial before an international tribunal.

2. The levels of administrative hierarchy in Rwanda (the *bourgmestres* or mayors, the armed forces, the militia heads, etc.). . . .

3. Those who profited from the situation and the general climate of violence, and apparent impunity, to carry out particularly sadistic and odious acts. Whenever they can be identified, they should be brought to trial.

4. Finally, there are the thousands of people who represent the majority of the guilty but who killed out of fear, because they were ordered to do so or because they were caught up in that situation of collective murder created by the authorities and the militias. Everybody had to take part: carrying a stick to break a

Tutsi skull was a way of proving 'non-allegiance to the RPF'. Refusal to kill was likely to lead directly to being killed. But a crime remains a crime, even when it is committed under duress and every murderer should, in principle, have to face some kind of trial.

The fourth category, however, does present a problem: the numbers involved—tens of thousands of individuals—is so great that it would be administratively impossible to judge all of them. It is better to admit this from the start to avoid it being used as a major argument against actioning the first two categories. Although there were many Germans who were interned in concentration camps as early as 1933 because of their opposition to the rise of national socialism, the scale of that genocide would have been impossible if the Nazis had not been able to depend on the German people as a whole through the organised bureaucracy of the state, what [philosopher] Hannah Arendt describes as 'the rule of Nobody'. But this argument was never used to prevent the trials going ahead. The massacres of Jews, just like those of Tutsis, were committed anonymously and it would be very difficult, although there are exceptional cases, to attribute the murder to any one Tutsi or to any one Hutu in particular. But this anonymity also masks the seriousness of the crime, to avoid the questions concerning guilt and responsibility: in short, it enables behaviour as though nothing has happened. Not all the guilty were judged in Germany, but the most important thing is that some were: at least some of those responsible paid for their crime. The Nazi ideology was outlawed and those who supported it openly were forced out of official posts and excluded from political life in general.

BELGIUM, FRANCE AND THE UNITED STATES

Belgium, France and the United States must accept a degree of responsibility for this genocide. Belgium is responsible for having largely created the political antagonism between the Hutus and Tutsis and then transforming it into a racial problem which sowed the seeds of the present tragedy. France closed its eyes to the growing racism at the heart of the system and the increasing number of massacres over the past four years and continued to support the former regime to the bitter end. The subsequent actions of the French government to protect the Tutsis cannot balance out the weight of the past. The United States can be accused of not taking up its moral responsibility as the major world power, blocking the initiatives of UN Secretary-General Boutros Boutros-Ghali and preventing US officials from using the word genocide to sidestep the international obligation to intervene that recognition of the crime would have imposed. . . .

However, the very positive degree of humanitarian support given by many countries cannot absolve them of an abdication of responsible action. It is now up to the United States, Belgium, France and the other countries of the European Union to work towards bringing the criminals to trial and helping in the reconstruction of Rwanda. These are political responsibilities that must be acknowledged and accepted by countries, either in the light of their past role in Rwanda, or of their present world status.

PERIODICAL BIBLIOGRAPHY

The following articles have been selected to supplement the diverse views presented in this chapter. Addresses are provided for periodicals not indexed in the *Readers' Guide to Periodical Literature*, the *Alternative Press Index*, the *Social Sciences Index*, or the *Index to Legal Periodicals and Books*.

Victoria Brittain	"The Congo Quagmire," *World Press Review*, November 1998.
William F. Buckley Jr.	"On Being Involved with Mankind," *National Review*, December 23, 1996.
Christian Century	"Outrage, Inertia over Burundi Crisis," July 31–August 7, 1996.
E.M. Colini	"A Tutsi's Hope," *Christianity Today*, April 7, 1997.
Francis M. Deng	"Ethnicity: An African Predicament," *Brookings Review*, Summer 1997.
Howard W. French	"A Century Later, Letting Africans Draw Their Own Map," *New York Times*, November 23, 1997.
Gail Furman	"Keep UN Troops in Angola," *New York Times*, May 31, 1997.
David Gough	"A War of Neighbors," *Maclean's*, September 7, 1998.
Philip Gourevitch	"The Genocide Fax," *New Yorker*, May 11, 1998.
Mark N. Katz	"Africa's Dilemma: European Borders, Contested Rule," *Current History*, April 1995.
Ali A. Mazrui	"Should Africa Recolonize Itself?" *World Press Review*, May 1995.
James C. McKinley Jr.	"Searching in Vain for Rwanda's Moral High Ground," *New York Times*, December 21, 1997.
Clive Mutiso	"Tribalism: Raising Hope," *Time*, April 13, 1998.
Yahya Sadowski	"Ethnic Conflict," *Foreign Policy*, Summer 1998.
Tom Stacey	"African Realities," *National Review*, May 19, 1997.
Kevin Whitelaw	"A Mission for Africa," *U.S. News & World Report*, September 29, 1997.
Jim Wurst	"Small Weapons of Mass Destruction," *In These Times*, December 13, 1998.
Alan Zarembo	"Judgment Day: In Rwanda, 92,392 Genocide Suspects Await Trial," *Harper's*, April 1997.

CHAPTER 3

WHAT IS THE STATE OF HUMAN RIGHTS IN AFRICA?

CHAPTER PREFACE

In 1948 the General Assembly of the United Nations voted to approve the Universal Declaration of Human Rights. The proclamation posited certain "fundamental human rights" to be "a common standard of achievement for all peoples and all nations." Among the rights listed were freedom of thought, expression, and assembly, freedom from slavery, torture, and arbitrary detention, and government based on "universal and equal suffrage." That same year, South Africa—one of eight nations to abstain from voting approval of the declaration—instigated a policy of apartheid. Its minority white population who controlled the government passed laws separating the nation's racial groups and restricting the voting and political rights of nonwhites. Government police powers were extended, opposition figures were imprisoned, press freedoms were suppressed, and political demonstrations were violently broken up.

South Africa's apartheid policy was unique to the continent, but its poor human rights record was not. In 1948 much of Africa was under the colonial control of European powers. During the 1950s and 1960s many colonies became free nations, but human rights expectations raised by independence were soon disappointed by adverse political developments including military coups, ethnic conflicts, and the rise of dictatorships. "By 1989, just seven of the forty-five states in sub-Saharan Africa preserved even the vestiges of democracy," writes historian John Reader. "Democracy had been stifled by military rule, as in Nigeria, or abandoned in favour of one-party systems, as in Kenya and the Ivory Coast, for example, where heads of state transformed themselves into presidents-for-life and politicians voicing opposition were locked up (or worse)."

The decade of the 1990s brought renewed hope concerning human rights and democracy to the continent. Several nations, such as Zambia and Malawi, held elections that turned long-time dictators out of office. Leaders of other African countries, notably Yoweri Museveni of Uganda, rejected multiparty democracy yet gained international recognition for supporting greater political and economic freedoms for their people. Perhaps most notably, South Africa abandoned its system of apartheid, legitimized opposition groups, and, in 1994, held political elections open to all races for the first time. Whether these developments signify a lasting positive human rights trend on the continent remains to be seen. The viewpoints in this chapter examine selected facets of the human rights situation in Africa.

"Democracy is an increasingly established fact in parts of the continent, and the potential of its emergence elsewhere is greater than ever before."

AFRICA IS MOVING TOWARD DEMOCRACY

David F. Gordon

David F. Gordon is a senior fellow of the Overseas Development Council, an international policy research institute. He previously worked as an advisor for the U.S. Agency for International Development (USAID) in Kenya, helping to promote democracy in that nation. In the following viewpoint, he argues that since the end of the Cold War between the United States and the Soviet Union in 1990, Africa has undergone many changes. These include the coming to power of a new generation of pragmatic and dynamic leaders and an evolution towards democracy in many parts of the continent. Gordon contends that while most African states cannot yet be described as fully democratic, Africa's democratization is a long-term process that the United States should continue to support.

As you read, consider the following questions:

1. Why have positive developments in Africa gone unnoticed elsewhere, according to Gordon?
2. Who does Gordon include as being one of Africa's "New Leaders?"
3. What recommendations does the author make for U.S. policy towards Africa?

Excerpted from David F. Gordon's testimony before the U.S. Senate Committee on Foreign Relations, Subcommittee on Africa, March 12, 1998.

Events on the ground in Africa and new political initiatives in this country are reshaping U.S.–Africa relations and creating new possibilities for more productive engagement. Africa is in the midst of profound change, and America's opportunity to affect these transitions and promote democracy and development has perhaps never been better. . . .

The tidal wave of change which swept over Europe at the end of the Cold War rippled across Africa as well. While the transformation has not been as sudden or dramatic as in Europe, the changes have been equally profound. Long-suppressed political energies have been released and old alliances have been re-ordered. Several longstanding civil conflicts have been resolved. In some countries, new forms of conflict have been released. But, perhaps most importantly, a new style of leadership has emerged. This new generation of leaders is more independent, more assertive, unfettered by the blinders of Cold War ideology, and pragmatically committed to economic and political reform. While changes are evident across virtually the entire continent, they are most striking and challenging in the Horn of Africa and the Great Lakes States—although I should hasten to add that by "the Great Lakes States," I refer to the likes of Uganda and Rwanda and not Vermont.

THE AFRICAN BALANCE SHEET

To many, the budding of democracy and economic rebirth in Africa has gone unnoticed: through the eyes of the media, images of political and economic trends on the African continent are overwhelmingly negative. War, famine and chaos appear to be the order of the day. The collapse of the Mobutu Sese Seko regime in Zaire, the toppling of the elected president in the neighboring Republic of Congo, continued ethnic conflict and tension in Rwanda and Burundi, the overthrow of a recently elected government in Sierra Leone, and deadly political strife in Kenya all made their way into the headlines in 1997.

But the media ignore much of the current reality in Africa. Good things are happening in Africa in addition to the not so good; and not in isolated instances. On the whole, Africa is better off, both economically and politically, than it was at the end of the Cold War, when the U.S. began earnest effort to promote economic and political reform. The continent is no longer an unvariegated wasteland of kleptocratic regimes, turmoil, and economic stagnation. While we cannot ignore the persistence of failed states such as Somalia, nor oppressive authoritarian rule as in Nigeria and the Sudan, nor continual ethnic conflict and political unrest in parts of Central Africa, all African countries must not be lumped together and pronounced disasters. . . .

Since 1990, more than three dozen African states have conducted multi-party elections, reflecting significant political liberalization and democratization across the continent. While elections are the most visible manifestations of democratization, equally important are significant improvements in the rule of law, civil liberties—particularly the strengthening of civil society and the reemergence of a free press—and a decline in human rights abuses. It is important, however, to stress that democratization is a long-term project in Africa, as it has been everywhere. African countries that have embarked upon democracy are generally in the early stages of democratization—the transition from authoritarian rule. Many have what might be called "hybrid" regimes, which combine democratic and nondemocratic elements. They are not yet consolidated democracies. . . .

Perhaps most importantly, there is a new generation emerging all over Africa that is committed to a new vision of the continent and its place in the world. This emerging cadre of African leaders—be they in government, the private sector or other sections of civil society—have been heavily influenced by the technological revolution and the global trends towards democratic governance and market-based, private sector focused economic policies. They eschew ideology and grand visions, and are oriented towards pragmatism and problem-solving. Many have spent a good deal of time overseas, most often in the West, and seek to translate effectively the benefits of global technology and culture into their local idioms.

AFRICA'S "NEW LEADERS"

Who are these "New Leaders?" If one includes the leaders of all African countries that have experienced a change of government or regime since 1990, the list of "New Leaders" would number over thirty, and include such dissimilar individuals as Charles Taylor of Liberia, Nigeria's Sani Abacha, Zambian Frederick Chiluba and South Africa's Nelson Mandela, leaders with little in common in terms of their personal agendas or visions for their countries or for Africa.

A different definition of "New Leaders" focuses on the broad generational change described above. And when foreign policy pundits talk about "the New Leaders of Africa" they tend to focus on four or five individuals who rule in Central Africa or the Horn: Meles Zanawi of Ethiopia, Isaias Afeworki of Eritrea, Yoweri Museveni of Uganda, Paul Kagame of Rwanda and (perhaps)

Laurent Kabila of the Congo.

Attention has focused on these five because of the assertive attitude they have taken towards the outside world and their willingness to engage forcefully in regional affairs, such as the overthrow of President Mobutu of Zaire. Some hail them as the new saviors of Africa; others condemn them as little more than a modernized version of Africa's traditional autocratic "big men."

I discount both of these views, and believe that a more nu-

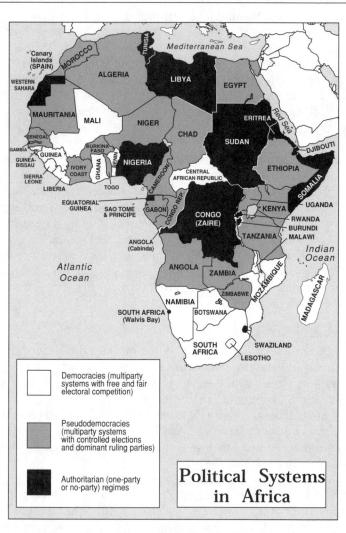

Source: Information compiled May 1998. Adapted from Larry Diamond, *Developing Democracy: Toward Consolidation* (Baltimore: Johns Hopkins University Press, forthcoming).

anced understanding of these "New Leaders" must inform U.S.–Africa policy.

What really sets this group apart is not their "newness" or what they are for, but what they are against. For these "New Leaders" the struggle is not against neo-colonialism or imperialism, but against tribalism and corruption. They have inherited nations devastated by corrupt, statist autocrats who wrecked their economies and impoverished the citizenry. All are committed to sweeping away the failures of the past including the political class associated with these failures in their respective countries. . . .

The conventional wisdom about the New Leaders is that all have embraced economic reform, re-established political stability and reduced human rights abuses, but resisted multi-party democracy, and that this strategy has achieved dramatic results. As such, they deserve, and indeed have received, the support of the international community because they are truly committed to putting their own houses in order.

A Closer Inspection

But on closer inspection, one also finds considerable variation among the chosen five. First of all, the so-called "new" leaders of Africa are not all new. Museveni has been in office for more than a decade; Meles and Isaias are approaching seven years. While Kabila is new in power, he represents a political style that harks back to earlier generations of African leaders.

In respect to economic reform and the establishment of a strong free market economy, while all are pragmatic and have given up most of what was an earlier commitment to Marxism, only Museveni has really delivered a comprehensive set of economic reforms. The others, while they reject the old-state run economic model, retain the tendency to distrust the capitalists. The "New Leaders" do appear to all subscribe to the notion that economic development precedes democracy, and reject the view that democratization and development are mutually supportive processes that occur at roughly the same time.

On the dimension of political stability, only Isaias governs a truly stable country with a broad based political regime. While Meles, Isaias and Museveni have brought peace to their countries, they have not yet won legitimacy in large sections of the population. Kagame rules a country which remains at war, while Kabila has yet to re-establish a national political system for the Congo, and there are serious doubts whether he has the inclination to do so. . . .

The "New Leaders" also have very different attitudes towards democracy. While none are "democrats" in our sense of the term, democratization has proceeded in varying paces in several of the countries. Free and fair elections have been held in Uganda to return Museveni to power and elect a new parliament. Elections in Ethiopia have not been fully free, while Eritrea is for all practical purposes a one party state, albeit a popular one. In Rwanda and Congo, the ruling regimes have made verbal commitments to democratic elections, but political circumstances do not seem to be moving in that direction.

DEMOCRATIZATION AND U.S.–AFRICA POLICY

The mixed record of democratization in Africa and the emergence of regimes led by individuals who appear to be committed to effective governance and real economic development, but not necessarily Western-style democracy, has led some analysts and foreign policy makers to question the wisdom of democracy and democracy promotion as core themes of U.S.–Africa policy. The skepticism about prospects for democracy and democracy promotion is being generated by a curious convergence of perspectives between those who continue to view Africa as a continent of economic stagnation and war, and those who are inclined to gloss over the less-promising details of the African reality. . . .

The critics of U.S. efforts to promote democracy in Africa base their argument on a combination of four assumptions:

First, that the social and economic conditions in Africa are not propitious for the sustainability of democracy. . . .

Second, that economic development and the reconstitution of failed states—the preconditions for democracy—are advanced most rapidly by a period of enlightened authoritarian rule. . . .

Third, that aggressive promotion of democracy runs at cross-purposes with other, more important foreign policy goals, especially in Central Africa. These goals include the establishment of stable and effective governments; strengthening regional security arrangements, especially among the "frontline states" bordering Sudan; preventing the re-emergence of genocide, and more effectively integrating Africa into the global economy.

Fourth, that democracy promotion is an exercise of forcing Western values on Africa, a form of cultural imperialism that is both self-defeating (What is the point of holding an election if all that happens is one ethnic-based regime replaces another?) and is rejected by the "New Leaders" who are committed to finding their own forms of democracy. . . .

I believe that the new skepticism about democracy in Africa

and the four assumptions on which it is based are unwarranted and reflect a distorted understanding of the African experience.

Is successful economic development a precondition for democracy? In Africa, the return to economic growth has been inextricably linked to political reform. Most, albeit not all, of the countries that are now experiencing positive rates of economic growth are countries that have embarked on democratic transitions, or where there has been genuine political liberalization. This is not surprising given the failure of authoritarian rule to have a positive developmental impact for most of Africa's independence period. It has been asserted many times that economic reform and democratization cannot occur simultaneously, but that is precisely what has been happening all across the continent. Moreover, those countries which have made the strongest commitment to democracy and the rule of law—Botswana, Mauritius, South Africa and Ghana—have been among the most successful in attracting foreign direct investment to their non-mineral sectors. . . .

DEMOCRACY AND STABILITY

Does promoting democracy endanger more important U.S. security interests in Africa? Because neither economic development nor political stability are likely to occur in Africa without accountable and inclusive government, democratization, and particularly democratic consolidation, is a critical component of viable governance. The United States should therefore not back away from this process, but continue to nurture it. We must be careful not to lose sight of this reality where other foreign policy goals are at stake. This is particularly true in central Africa where the U.S. seeks to contain the Sudan, bring peace to the Great Lakes, and support the reconstruction of the Congo. While it is in our interest to work closely with Ethiopia and Uganda to deal with Sudan, the viability of such a policy is at risk so long as neither Meles nor Museveni preside over inclusive and stable polities. Similarly, in the Great Lakes, downplaying democratization in Rwanda and Congo risks putting the U.S. in a position of uncritical support of narrowly-based regimes that will not bring stability to these countries.

The choice between democracy promotion on the one hand, and a concern for regional stability on the other, is largely a false one. The U.S. can and should pursue both. This will no doubt create some tensions, but there is no reason to believe that promotion of democracy will undermine the bilateral relationship with the "New Leaders" or compromise other foreign policy goals. The "New Leaders" seek mature relations with the U.S., not the paternalism of the past. We should take the same approach towards them. Will Meles or Museveni not join with the U.S. to contain the Sudan because the U.S. continues to urge further democratization in their own interests. Will the vigorous promotion of democracy in these countries make life more complicated for our ambassadors there? Probably, but articulating the complexity and rationale for U.S. policy is what professional diplomats are paid to do.

DEMOCRACY AND AFRICAN VALUES

Is democracy a Western, alien value unsuited to African soil? In Africa, as elsewhere where democratization has been most vigorously resisted, the argument that democracy is an alien value is often merely a justification for the continuation of authoritarian rule. Indeed, this rhetoric harks back to the initial rejection of liberal democracy and the search for "African democracy" by the early architects of one-party rule during the 1960s such as Kwame Nkrumah in Ghana and Julius Nyerere in Tanzania. Those who argue that democratization in Africa is an alien imposition forget that the current demand for democracy across the continent has come primarily from within by those who challenged incumbent authoritarian regimes in the streets (e.g. in Benin, Ghana, Kenya, Nigeria, South Africa and Zaire). External actors played only a supportive role in the initiation of Africa's recent political evolution.

If allowed to determine U.S.–Africa policy, skepticism towards democracy and democratization will result in outcomes that are in neither the U.S. nor Africa's interest. In particular, stepping away from a commitment to democracy in Africa will lead the United States back to a Cold War-like policy of supporting regimes out of short-term tactical considerations. Such a policy will undermine Africa's democratic forces, and result in less rather than more progress on political consolidation, conflict resolution and economic development. Having become serious about democratization since the end of the Cold War, are we to retreat from this goal just when the policy of its promotion is bearing fruit? I submit that the answer should be an emphatic "no."

The failure to stay the course in respect to democracy promotion also risks abandoning those individuals and groups that have fought hard to bring democracy to their countries. . . . This will undermine the credibility of past and current policies in such countries as Kenya where we have worked hard to nurture a democratic transition in the face of a hostile regime, but where much progress in the form of a vibrant civil society and the beginning of constitutional reform, has nonetheless been made. It may also generate a backlash against the U.S. and other Western governments from Africa's democrats.

DEALING WITH THE "NEW LEADERS"

At the center of the debate about democracy in U.S.–Africa policy is the question of what approach the U.S. should take towards the "New Leaders" in the Great Lakes and the Horn of Africa. . . .

I believe that we should be broadly encouraging and supportive of the "New Leaders." While these individuals are not as morally compelling as Nelson Mandela, they do bring a new courage, a new energy and a new honesty to the African scene. But at the same time, we must keep our eyes open and treat them as mature partners, calling them to account when they err, but in a manner that is mindful that we do not have a monopoly on wisdom.

We need to be particularly concerned that the political scene in all of these countries remains dominated by individuals rather than institutions. Continued restrictions on civil society combined with limitations on multipartyism will make real accountability ultimately impossible. The "New Leaders" rule over regimes that are brittle and thus vulnerable. They are likely to evolve either into more inclusive—and more democratic—polities or slip back into the forms of authoritarian rule that characterized Africa throughout the 1980s. And such a return to authoritarianism with its attendant loss of legitimacy risks state collapse and civil war. That is why it is important for the United States to maintain a focus on democracy as a goal of its policy and diplomacy in these states. That is also why democratization is in the self-interest of those in power. . . .

UGANDA AND GHANA

Consider the particular case of U.S. policy toward Uganda. Some argue that the U.S. should not push Museveni to deepen the democratization process, either because authoritarianism is just what Uganda needs, or because Museveni has already put Uganda on the path toward democracy, albeit one that differs from the Western model. What I am suggesting is that, while broadly cooperating with and supporting the Museveni regime, the U.S. should maintain a significant dialogue and program about the need to deepen the democratization process in Uganda in order to sustain that country's remarkable progress. Issues to be addressed might include: strengthening the rule of law and transparency and accountability of government, making decentralization meaningful, and ensuring electoral competition no matter what political framework the country adopts.

Can such a policy work? In looking at how to approach the "New Leaders" in the Great Lakes and the Horn, U.S. policy makers need to review their experience in dealing with a similar figure in West Africa, Ghana's Jerry Rawlings. In the late 1980s, Rawlings, who had come to power through a military coup, undertook a tough economic reform program with support of the International Monetary Fund (IMF) and the World Bank. The U.S. strongly supported this effort, but continued to engage the Rawlings regime with the need to move to a more open and broad-based political system, echoing the views of Ghana's strongly democratic middle class.

THE GROWTH OF DEMOCRACY IN AFRICA

Democracy is ascendant as many African countries undertake significant political reforms. During the last decade, the number of democracies in sub-Saharan Africa has grown fivefold. While the democratization process has not been as far-reaching as it could be and there have been setbacks, some 25 African states now enjoy a democratic form of government.

Susan Rice, address before African Studies Association, November 14, 1998.

In the early 1990s, Rawlings established a multi-party system, but the first elections, held in 1992, failed to win the legitimacy of large segments of the population. In response, the U.S., while continuing its support of the Rawlings government, engaged with the Ghanaian Opposition to explore means of bringing them back into the political process. This led a very large and multi-year effort by USAID to improve the electoral machinery in Ghana. Ghana's second elections were held in 1996. While the outcome was quite similar to the first, this time they gained broad legitimacy and have led to the active participation of the opposition in parliament and a broad and open political debate about a wide range of issues.

By having a steady policy of engagement with a dynamic new leader, but not losing sight of the importance of political reform and democratization to sustain economic policy reforms and growth, the U.S. played a positive role in Ghana's evolution. Many of today's "New Leaders" in the Great Lakes and the Horn have political views similar to Rawlings' seven or eight years ago. We should shape an approach to them that learns from our successful experiences in Ghana. . . .

Sustaining this dimension of U.S. foreign policy is critical at the very time when democracy is an increasingly established fact in parts of the continent, and the potential of its emergence elsewhere is greater than ever before. The arrival of Africa's "New Leaders" represents an historic opportunity for the continent. Africa's cycles of despair can be broken. But it will require a commitment to vision, engagement and pragmatism by our leaders in the promotion of democracy in Africa.

| "Elections in *Africa are easily and often stolen, and in many cases serve to allow dictators and military thugs to wrap themselves in a cloak of legitimacy."

AFRICA'S RULERS DO NOT SUPPORT DEMOCRACY

Keith B. Richburg

Keith B. Richburg is a journalist for the *Washington Post* who was stationed in Africa from 1991 to 1994. In the following viewpoint, adapted from his 1997 book *Out of America: A Black Man Confronts Africa*, Richburg examines the "new breed" of African leaders who came into power in the 1990s and who have been praised as being more democratic and less corrupt than their predecessors. Richburg argues that these leaders are just as autocratic as the dictators that preceded them. Much change is required for African nations to become truly democratic, he contends, including reducing government control over the media and security forces, intensively monitoring elections, and rewriting existing state constitutions.

As you read, consider the following questions:

1. Why does the holding of elections not always signify true democracy in Africa, according to Richburg?
2. Why, in the author's view, should African nations consider peaceful means of breaking up and coming together?
3. What role, according to Richburg, should the United States play in the political evolution of Africa?

Reprinted from Keith B. Richburg, "The More Things Change," *The New Republic*, June 16, 1997, by permission of *The New Republic*; ©1997 by The New Republic, Inc.

Can a onetime Marxist guerrilla use free-market capitalism to restructure his country's shattered economy? That question, the lead-in to an article I wrote for the *Washington Post* in February 1992, was posed after a trip I took to Ethiopia and Eritrea, following interviews with the two countries' presidents, Meles Zenawi and Isaias Afwerki. Both were Marxist-inspired revolutionaries who went to the bush as young men a quarter-century ago, and who jettisoned socialism in the 1980s as they moved closer to toppling longtime dictator Mengistu Haile Mariam. And the same question can be asked five years later in 1997, about another successful guerrilla leader, Laurent Désiré Kabila, who has succeeded, against all expectations, in ousting the most entrenched of Africa's Big Men, Mobutu Sese Seko.

A NEW BREED OF LEADERS

Many have compared Kabila to his chief backers—Uganda's Yoweri Museveni, another former guerrilla commander who has emerged as the darling of the international community for reviving economic growth in that war-ravaged nation, and Paul Kagame, the architect of the Rwandan Patriotic Front's lightning victory over the Hutu regime in Kigali. Stretching both facts and logic, commentators have even termed these former bush fighters a kind of much needed "new breed" of African leaders—technocratic not tribal, more pragmatic than ideological, and able to speak the language of the World Bank and the international aid community.

But that is far too rosy. Museveni and Kagame are autocratic figures who brook no opposition and seem more comfortable with the strict military chain of order and command than with the compromise of politics. Kabila, who has renamed Zaire the Democratic Republic of the Congo, has already displayed a notably undemocratic streak, barring all elections for two years, suspending all political activity and criminalizing the act of forming a political party, creating a cabinet that excludes some of the key politicians who opposed Mobutu's regime and, in his latest move, banning miniskirts and tight trousers for Congolese women.

And what has been the international community's response to this new kind of African Big Man? At this point: silence. In many ways, the West, including the United States, seems as willing to tolerate these new "benign" autocrats as they were to embrace their more ruthless predecessors. The old litmus test for Western support was anticommunism; the new version is free-market principles and structural adjustment programs.

By embracing these new autocrats, rather than using aid as a carrot to force democratic reforms, the United States may be squandering its leverage. That's partly the result of an incoherent Africa policy reduced to a series of ad hoc reactions to crises on the ground. By failing to act more forcefully to facilitate dictators' exits from the scene, Washington policymakers surrender the stage to guerrilla leaders who fight their way in from the bush and whose victories embolden them—and make them more resistant to outside pressure. Mobutu will certainly not be the last of the Big Men to fall in this way. Another candidate is Kenya's Daniel arap Moi, widely expected to manipulate his way back into power by rigging elections late in 1997. [Editor's note: Moi was reelected president in elections held in December 1997.] In 1992, writing about Zaire in the Washington Post, I said: "Amid the stalemate, analysts say, some Zaireans may consider abandoning their peaceful struggle for democracy and launching a guerrilla war to oust Mobutu." It seemed far-fetched then, just as it seems far-fetched for Kenya today. But it may well come to pass there, as it came to pass in Zaire, unless aggressive, preventive diplomacy forces a managed transition to democracy.

BUILDING DEMOCRACY IN AFRICA

But building democracy in Africa is not a simple proposition. For a start, Western policymakers must recognize that in Africa the holding of elections does not necessarily mean true democracy—in many cases, the exact opposite holds true. Elections in Africa are easily and often stolen, and in many cases serve to allow dictators and military thugs to wrap themselves in a cloak of legitimacy.

Zambia, for example, held elections in November 1996, but the country is far from "democratic" in the sense that the opposition is allowed to freely compete, and the press is free of harassment. Sierra Leone held a democratic election in 1996, but the soldiers seized power again in yet another coup against weak civilian rule. Elsewhere on the continent, soldiers who have taken power through coups have staged, and won, dubious elections, as occurred in December 1996 in Ghana. In South Korea, former military leaders have been put on trial and imprisoned; in Africa, they simply change into civilian garb, proclaim their newfound faith in democracy, and get themselves "elected."

Before truly democratic African countries can hold truly democratic elections, there is an immense amount that needs to happen: constitutions must be rewritten to reduce the power of imperial presidencies and to level the playing field for opposition parties. Government control over the media must be broken, and that especially applies to the state-run radio stations on which most rural Africans depend for their news. Security and police forces, mostly tools of repression, need to be brought under neutral command and control. Fair and impartial election laws must be drafted. Voters must be properly registered and opposition parties given the voters' lists and the locations of polling places well in advance. Mechanisms must be put in place to monitor funding, to prevent entrenched Big Men from simply printing more money to buy more votes. Laws that now make it a crime to "insult" the president must be repealed so opposition candidates feel free to engage in vigorous debate. Voter education drives need to be conducted. And election losers must be given a constitutional role, and thus a stake in the outcome, so that elections no longer become the kind of "winner-take-all" contests that lead to factional warfare. International election monitoring groups also need to get involved much earlier, and on a far wider scale, instead of parachuting into African countries a few days before the votes are cast.

Gado/*Daily Nation*/Nairobi. Reprinted by permission of Cartoonists & Writers Syndicate.

Here, the continent might take a lesson from South Africa, which went through a lengthy process of constitutional revision that laid the groundwork for the eventual, successful, democratic transition. In fact, Nelson Mandela and the African National Congress resisted demands, even from some of the ANC's own supporters, to rush headlong into elections before constitutional arrangements were in place.

But African countries have a problem that runs even deeper than bad government: state illegitimacy. Most of the civil wars and conflicts around the continent are, in some form or another, caused by separatist sentiment, with one ethnic group fearing domination by another. In Somalia, the civil war grinds on in Mogadishu because the two branches of the Hawiye clan, and the subfactions of the Habre Gedir, refuse to cede power or territory to perceived enemies from opposing clan and subclan factions. The minority Tutsi army in Burundi refuses to give any power away to the Hutu majority, and the minority Tutsi in Rwanda, mindful of the 1994 genocide, will not consider real power sharing with the defeated Hutu refugees and returnees. It goes on and on.

For the last three and a half decades, African strongmen have been content to sweep those secession claims under the carpet, or else ruthlessly suppress them. The Organization of African Unity (OAU) has even enshrined as one of its inviolable tenets the idea that the continent's old borders, drawn up arbitrarily by European colonizers, can never be altered. The fear is rational enough; recognizing the claim of any one group could lead to the chaos of conflicting claims. But the attitude is wrong and outdated, and needs to change if Africa is to have any chance at successfully burying its civil wars and entering the new global economic system. Here, Africans can look to the northeast corner of their continent, where, in 1993, little Eritrea broke off and became independent from Ethiopia, and Meles Zenawi's new government in Addis Ababa let it go without much fuss.

But if African countries should consider rational and peaceful ways of breaking up, they must also find new ways of coming together, through stronger regional and subregional groupings. These two ideas—African states breaking up and simultaneously coming together—are not as contradictory as they might appear. They are two halves of an evolutionary process that one scholar, Peter Lyon at the Institute of Commonwealth Studies in London, refers to as "Fission and Fusion."

"Fission" means that in the absence of any overarching ideology like the East-West rivalry, and as separatist sentiments come to the fore, peoples around the world are expressing more vocally their demands for autonomy and separate statehood. But, at the same time, these demands seem less dire than before as countries become more economically interlinked through groupings like the European Community, the Association of South East Asian Nations, and the like. Quebec might want to

Africa's New Generation of Leaders

The rise of a New Generation of African leaders is generally viewed as a positive development in Africa. Usually comprised of President Laurent Kabila of the Democratic Republic of Congo, Vice President Paul Kagame of Rwanda, President Yoweri Museveni of Uganda, Prime Minister Meles Zenawi of Ethiopia, and President Isaias Afwerki of Eritrea, the New Generation is best characterized by the pursuit of African solutions for African problems—a greater independence from the West and a less corrupt administration of their countries. . . .

I fear we will wake up in several years and find the New Generation of African leaders has become an old generation of African strongmen.

These leaders have done much for their countries, but all preside over de facto one-party states which do not allow for self-government and have not established mechanisms for the peaceful transfer of power. Political oppression, serious violations of civil liberties, and a restricted press are all elements of life in these countries. These leaders certainly have replaced some of the most corrupt and brutal governments in Africa, but their commitment to genuine political reform and governmental institution building still must be proven.

Senator John Ashcroft, March 12, 1998, statement.

---

separate from Canada, but the consequences of separation would be far less dramatic if an independent Quebec were still a member of the North American Free Trade Area. Eritrea and Ethiopia split, but the two are still closely tied by transport and trade links.

America's Role

What role can the United States and other Western countries play in building the conditions for regional integration, minority rights and real democracy? One way to start might be to end the annual donor game, where the international lending community insists on economic and political reforms as a condition of continued assistance, and dictators comply grudgingly, at the last minute, just before the aid money is cut off. The money flows for another six months or a year, and the old pattern of repression re-emerges, until the ritual is repeated all over again. Kenya's Moi has become the continent's virtuoso of the aid game; he has figured out exactly how much reform is enough to keep the donors happy. And he has also played on Western fears that authoritarian control is the only way to keep African states from falling apart. It's a seductive argument. Northeast from Kenya is Somalia, and northwest is Sudan, both wracked by long-running civil wars. With neighbors like that, Kenya and Moi actually start to look pretty good. This is what Mobutu said as well, and likely what Laurent Kabila will say, too. And so the tyrants whose brutal and impoverishing policies create the conditions for state collapse then use the specter of state collapse to procure the aid they need to hold onto power.

Will the second-term Clinton administration recognize that these Big Men—new breed or old—are not the solution but the problem, and that the stability they impart is illusory? Will it pursue preventive diplomacy to manage Africa's crises before the rebels pound at the capital gates? Or will policy remain reactive and ad hoc? If America's Africa policy continues along its current path, then the headlines and stories coming out of Africa in 2007 will likely be very much like those of 1997. The faces may change. The Big Men may be talking the language of free markets instead of the rhetoric of anticommunism. But Africa's problems will remain lamentably the same.

"*A written Constitution and Bill of Rights as protective as America's now defend South Africans against official abuse.*"

SOUTH AFRICA'S POST-APARTHEID GOVERNMENT PROTECTS HUMAN RIGHTS

Anthony Lewis

South Africa has been praised as an example of a successful and peaceful political transformation into a democratic society. From 1948 to 1991 its government practiced a policy of official racial segregation called apartheid (separateness). Whites controlled the government and denied nonwhites economic and political rights, including the right to vote. After years of international sanctions and internal unrest, the government repealed the laws underpinning apartheid in 1991. In 1994 in elections open to all races, Nelson Mandela—the head of South Africa's leading opposition group (the African National Congress) and a political prisoner from 1962 to 1990—was elected president. In the following viewpoint, Anthony Lewis writes that under Mandela's leadership, South Africa has created a new constitution and a new political culture with high respect for human rights. Lewis is a columnist for the *New York Times*.

As you read, consider the following questions:

1. What social problems continue to affect South Africa, according to Lewis?
2. How has Nelson Mandela transformed the political landscape of South Africa in a way that enhances respect for human rights, in the author's view?

Excerpted from Anthony Lewis, "Mandela the Pol," *The New York Times*, March 23, 1997; ©1997 by The New York Times. Reprinted with permission.

When I began visiting South Africa 30 years ago, it was a police state that enforced official racism with a mad logic. Government employees classified people as white or colored (mixed race) by testing the curl in their hair. Hundreds of thousands of blacks were arrested every year for being in a "white area" without the right pass. Sex across color lines was a crime. A teen-age boy was sentenced to five years in prison under the Terrorism Act for writing an anti-white poem and "publishing" it by showing it to his girlfriend.

I thought then, and on many later visits, that South Africa was the most fascinating country on earth. There were exceptional human beings—bishops and writers and lawyers and political thinkers—whose struggle against the system seemed to deepen their characters. And there was a great unfinished drama. How long could whites, then 16 percent of the population, continue to hold all political and economic power? Would it end in an explosion, or would there somehow be a peaceful transition to majority rule? Richard Rive, a colored literary scholar, put it in a sentence to me in 1975: "The end is inevitable, but not predictable."

To revisit the country now is a dazzling experience. The old sense of entering a vast prison is gone. There are no restraints on what political creed one may espouse. No one is "banned" or held in detention without trial. Life in South Africa is a human kaleidoscope of colors: in shops and business offices and not least in Parliament, that former bastion of whiteness. And at the center, where for two generations stern Afrikaner leaders enforced the ideology of racial separation, stands the benign, all-embracing figure who brought about the peaceful transformation, President Nelson Mandela.

A REVERED FIGURE

Mandela is probably the most widely known political leader in the world, and without doubt the most revered. In an age of ethnic, religious and racial conflicts, societies of a very different character and history wish they had someone of his unifying qualities and unassailable standing; I have heard that from, among others, Israelis and Palestinians. He is one of the most written-about figures anywhere. . . .

Yet in profound respects Mandela remains a mystery. What exactly is the magic of his leadership, the means by which he persuades diverse people in what was a riven country to join with him? What enabled him to survive 27 years in prison without disabling bitterness? What makes him Mandela?

The South African drama continues, the fascination of its central character undiminished. Now Mandela is coming under criticism for his Government's performance; people are asking whether the qualities that enabled him to lead the country peacefully to freedom are right for the fretful business of governing. So I found on a visit in February 1997 to explore the Mandela mystery. . . .

I talked with President Mandela in the presidential residence outside Cape Town. The house used to be called Westbrooke; two years ago he renamed it Genadendal, as a symbol of South Africa's diversity and unity. Genadendal was a Christian mission established in 1738, the oldest in South Africa; it was a sanctuary for former slaves after the abolition of slavery, and in Genadendal the Dutch dialect arose that helped to form the Afrikaans language. . . .

The interview took place at 7 in the morning, in an alcove looking out across beautiful lawns and trees down the hill toward Rondebosch, a suburb that is the home of the University of Cape Town. The President came down after having breakfast in his room upstairs. No security men were in sight until an hour later.

I began by asking about the future, about where South Africa was headed. But seven years after his release from prison in 1990, with a new Constitution in place and himself in office after the country's first democratic election, he was still concerned about national unity. He wanted to talk first about the peaceful transformation. South Africa, he said, had avoided "tragedies such as Bosnia."

What lessons, I asked, did he think the South African story had for Bosnia and other conflicted societies? "It would be presumptuous of me to lecture" Bosnian leaders, he answered. But then he added: "They thought through their blood and not through their brains. In countries where innocent people are dying, the leaders are following their blood rather than their brains."

It was a rare piece of self-revelation, I thought. The world sees Nelson Mandela as a man of extraordinary magnanimity, eschewing revenge for the cruelties of apartheid, reaching out to enemies: the nearest thing politics has to a saint. True, but not the whole truth. When you talk to those who know him best, you come to understand that Mandela is anything but benign. He is a man of powerful emotions but even more powerful discipline. If he is saintly, he is saintly for a purpose. Through 27 years of prison and now 7 of public leadership, he has disciplined himself to suppress his feelings: to think with his brains and not his blood. . . .

STEVE BIKO

To carry out the Mandela theme of reconciliation, not revenge, his new Government as one of its first acts set up a Truth and Reconciliation Commission with power to grant amnesty to individuals in return for full confession of a political crime. When I talked with the President, the commission had just received amnesty applications from five former policemen involved in what was probably the single most notorious apartheid killing: the murder of Steve Biko, the young Black Consciousness movement leader who died of brain damage while he was in jail in 1977. At the time, under oath, the police denied responsibility for his death. Now they said they had killed him inadvertently. The extent and truth of their confessions must be tested at hearings where in other cases, the details were so gruesome that the commission chairman, retired Archbishop Desmond Tutu, put his head down on the table and wept.

I asked the President whether the public would continue to support the policy of amnesty as the horrifying truth of what happened to Steve Biko and others came out. "In fact," he answered, "some of the relatives of the victims have said, 'We don't want revenge, but we want to know what happened to our beloveds.' And that is an indication. If a person who has actually suffered can say that, then you know people understand that you can't build a united nation on the basis of revenge."

Mandela never met Steve Biko, who rose to prominence while Mandela was in prison; Biko's name is not mentioned in his autobiography. Biko led a movement whose first premise, at least—that blacks should rely on themselves for liberation—was very different from the A.N.C.'s historic nonracialism. I asked the President what role he thought Biko would have played if he had lived.

"There can be no doubt that he was one of the most talented and colorful freedom fighters South Africa has produced," he said. Then he placed Biko in his own pantheon of unity. "Young as he was, he was concerned with the question of unity. . . . Now that is a young man with realism, who could at that stage have felt that we were wasting our energies, our talents, by remaining divided."

A realist: Mandela's highest praise. Neville Alexander, his fellow prisoner, said Mandela's realism was the more effective because he was "extremely patient and wise. He's always been prepared to wait for people to catch up with reality. We wanted to fight the prison authorities. He said, 'Look, chaps, we're going to be here 10 years or more.'"

MANDELA'S GOALS

Alexander's view of Mandela, in the testing conditions of Robben Island, is especially interesting because his politics were different. He was a Marxist with a Ph.D. from Tubingen University in Germany, a member not of the African National Congress but of a university group called the National Liberation Front. He spoke with admiration of Mandela's single-minded pragmatic leadership even though the two men were ideologically apart in prison and, according to others, were on cool terms personally.

"His goal always was the deracialization of South African society and the creation of a liberal democracy," Alexander said. "For that end he was willing to make compromises with people of different views. He was able to concentrate on his goal with utter conviction and lucidity, and he was a man of extreme discipline. His aristocratic family background and training—one can use that term realistically—were reinforced by both legal practice and a jurisprudential cast of mind."

Helen Suzman, who as an opposition member of Parliament visited the prisoners on Robben Island starting in 1967, said the same thing about Mandela's consistent goal: "'I want to normalize things in South Africa.' That was what he always said to me in prison." What really mattered was ending the racial supremacy that dominated the country's life. Everything else—economic theory, social ideology—was subordinated in his mind to that end. . . .

In his character and his place in his country's history, Mandela brings to mind George Washington. Of course they are worlds apart, in time and culture. But Washington's biographers, too, describe him as a man of strong emotions who suppressed them in the interest of creating a nation. His disciplined leadership held the quarreling colonies together in war and kept such strong-minded political antagonists as Thomas Jefferson and Alexander Hamilton together in his Cabinet.

"There is in the life of a country but one such person; we are just lucky that he came along at this time." That was said to me of Mandela by his lawyer, George Bizos. It sounds like the standard appraisal of Washington. The face that Washington presented to the world was not Mandela's disarming smile but an austere formality. But the two seem similar in the controlled personalities that made them the irreplaceable fathers of their countries.

A GREAT PRESIDENT?

The question emerging in South Africa is whether the Great Reconciler is also a great President. In Washington's day there was world enough and time. In Mandela's, South Africans, like everyone else, have to compete pell-mell in a world economy. A fast-growing population suffers from unemployment that may be as high as 40 percent, a grotesquely unequal distribution of wealth, appalling crime. Voices are beginning to be heard complaining about Mandela's record on those and other problems.

"The young are fed up," a prominent black figure told me, "with 400,000 coming on the job market every year and few jobs. They think this old man has been too much of a moderate, too reconciliatory, too compromising." Kaizer Nyatsumba, political editor of *The Star* in Johannesburg, wrote a tough column after Mandela denounced some black journalists. "His unquestionable greatness notwithstanding," Nyatsumba said, "Mandela is an ordinary man with feet of clay."

THREE REFORM PROCESSES

South Africa is going through three reform processes simultaneously: democratization, de-racialization, and development. The African National Congress (ANC) inherited a closed system of government typical of a police state. Now the watchwords are accountability, transparency, and good governance, and the ANC has made huge strides in bringing them into play.

Jonathan Steele, *World Press Review*, August 1997.

If one ranks the challenges facing South Africa by what is on people's minds, crime is the most serious. Across lines of race and class, it is the subject of conversation. Carjacking is a terrifying example. Drivers are jumped as they get into their cars outside their homes or stop at a red light, ordered out at gunpoint, sometimes killed. . . . "The main problem in the country is criminal violence," said Winston Floquet, the chief executive of Fleming Martin Securities. His brother-in-law was shot dead outside his home, and two people in Floquet's office were attacked recently. One of them immediately left for Australia. White emigration has increased, and Floquet said Australians are vigorously recruiting South African financial professionals.

When I asked President Mandela about crime, he began by saying, "We don't want to be complaining about what happened under the apartheid regime—we have now been in power for more than two and one-half years, and it is our responsibility to solve problems as we find them." But it is a reality, he said, that in the apartheid years the police concentrated "not on detecting crime but on suppressing political activity." Others of varying political views made the same point to me. Not only did the white police devote most of their effort to putting down dissent; they also encouraged black policemen in Soweto to make deals with criminal syndicates that let the criminals operate in return for their help in the job of suppression. So corruption was and is a major problem. The President said his Government had arrested more police on corruption charges in its brief life than previous Governments had in the 45 years of apartheid: 400 police in the Johannesburg area alone.

The apartheid system did create conditions for crime: oppressive racial discrimination, deliberate denial of decent education to blacks, miserable housing and economic policies that left millions jobless. But the President was right that the responsibility is his Government's now, and its performance so far has to be judged a failure. In his address at the opening of Parliament in Cape Town last month he said, "Let me warn the criminals—the carjackers, the rapists—we will make their lives difficult." Perhaps new policies will take hold, but the police are still undermanned and underreformed.

HOUSING

Housing is a signal disappointment in the Government's record. The need is overwhelming, as even a casual visitor who looks around will understand. On the way to town from the Cape Town Airport you pass Crossroads, a squatter community that became famous 20 years ago, when the apartheid Government bulldozed it, not just once but repeatedly. But the squatter problem persisted, as thousands of blacks fled the desolate "homelands" to which they were confined under apartheid. It is still not over. From time to time, residents of Crossroads are resettled, but new thousands move in and build their shacks. And not just in Crossroads. Around the country homeless families occupy land—often land on which the Government plans to build houses. It is a serious enough problem that President Mandela, in his speech at the opening of Parliament last month, condemned the illegal "occupation of land."

The A.N.C. promised in the 1994 election campaign to build a million new homes in five years; so far, according to the Department of Housing, 123,000 have been built or are under construction. On the plus side, millions of people have been provided clean water and electricity for the first time. Mandela estimated that 1.7 million more would get water this year: a remarkable accomplishment.

The contrast between Cape Town, which may be the most

beautiful city in the world, and nearby Crossroads symbolizes a fundamental truth about South Africa. It is both a first- and a third-world country, with some people, most of them whites, living in a luxury scarcely matched anywhere else, and others barely surviving. The society's gross disparities in wealth remain essentially untouched, a time bomb for possible future social turmoil.

When I asked Mandela about that, he said: "We must not overestimate the speed with which a democratic government can bring about change in the thinking of the community or the structure of the economy. We are determined not to be deflected from the aim of assuring that there's a proper distribution. But we must not be unrealistic. We want to bring about change without any dislocation to the economy." He added that a start had been made on equalizing wages and on what is called black economic empowerment, black ownership of major companies. A striking example of the latter is the move by Cyril Ramaphosa, who was the A.N.C.'s chief constitutional negotiator, from politician to capitalist as the head of a large industrial group.

Mandela's caution about "dislocation to the economy" reflects a big change in his thinking and that of his colleagues, a growing concern about killing the golden goose in pursuit of equality. The A.N.C.'s 1955 Freedom Charter called for nationalization in some areas of the economy, and that was still in the air in 1990. The word is not heard today. When I spoke with the President, one of the first statements he volunteered was, "Private sector development remains the motive force of growth and development."

Leaders of business say they are content with the Government. Bobby Godsell, a high executive in the giant Anglo American Corporation, said he was "robustly optimistic." His reason was that "at long last the fundamental diseases of the economy are being tackled." From the mid-1970's on, the apartheid Government ran very high budget deficits. The effect, Godsell said, was "to depress saving and investment, which undermined our capacity to acquire new technology, to be globally competitive." Helen Suzman, one of the sharpest critics around, said: "You cannot undo 45 years of misgovernance in so short a time. In that light they've done amazingly well."....

The question is what the orthodox economic policy being followed by the Government will do to meet the expectations of the poor majority of blacks, and how soon. Mandela was careful not to raise expectations high in the 1994 election campaign. And South Africans have always been patient—astonishingly so by American standards. Will that patience continue? Deputy President Mbeki has said that it will if people can see some improvement, however modest: a fresh water tap, a halt to the eviction of rural tenants. The Government aims to raise the economic growth rate to 6 percent. But that will take lots of foreign investment, which has not flooded in so far, and an increase in worker skills.

EDUCATION

"The worst legacy of apartheid is the lack of education," Winston Floquet said. "People say South Africa is going to be another tiger economy, like the ones in Asia. But you can't get there from such a low skills base. It will haunt us for at least another decade."

Segregated schools and grossly disproportionate spending on white students played a key part in creating the separate worlds that the philosophers of apartheid wanted. But that is changing rapidly, as large numbers of black children enroll in the once all-white public schools in the suburbs of Johannesburg. "It is one of the most successful pieces of racial integration that I know about in the world," Bobby Godsell said. "It is one area in which the two worlds have begun to overlap."

But around the country most black children still get a sadly inadequate education. And critics say the Government is leveling down rather than up. It set a national standard of 1 teacher to 40 pupils and then forced thousands of teachers in Western Cape Province to move or retire because the ratio there was only 1 to 25 or 30. (Almost all retired.)

CRITICISMS OF THE GOVERNMENT

Beyond these specific areas of doubt about the Mandela Government's performance, there is criticism about the way it governs. The complaint is that the President is too autocratic, too loyal to failed Cabinet ministers who go into a defensive crouch when their mistakes are exposed. Dr. Mamphela Ramphele, vice chancellor of the University of Cape Town, and a close friend of Mandela, said: "The more insecure people are, the less open they are to constructive criticism. He's not insecure, but his Government is."

Some of Mandela's old A.N.C. colleagues have been successes in office, others surely not. . . .

There are questions, too, about the way President Mandela has anointed Thabo Mbeki as his successor. . . .

Finally, among the felt doubts about Mandela as President, there is a concern that he has carried his emphasis on unity too far, to the point of dampening the criticism that characterizes democracy. . . .

Those are the main criticisms of Nelson Mandela as President. To me, they are overshadowed—overwhelmed—by his achievements in the last three years. He has taken a country utterly divided by race and made it one where people of different races actually share a vision: where "the two worlds have begun to overlap," as Bobby Godsell of Anglo American put it. He has transformed the political system without creating unrealistic expectations in the newly enfranchised. He has taken a country where fear was everywhere and made it free. He has given a society marked by official murder a culture of human rights.

I find South Africans today less resentful, less guilty, less prickly about race than many Americans. The submissiveness of some blacks is fading along with white lordliness. Young black lawyers call senior white colleagues by their first names: a social revolution.

A HUMAN RIGHTS CULTURE

But it is the acceptance of a human rights culture that struck me most powerfully on this visit. Law used to be an instrument of oppression. It dictated where you could live, whom you could marry, what you could read. The masters of that system rejected all demands for legal protection of individual rights, and many feared that when change came the new masters would be as unrelenting toward the old. But Mandela the lawyer, together with Cyril Ramaphosa and Arthur Chaskalson and George Bizos and other lawyers, carried out a revolution by law and in law.

A written Constitution and Bill of Rights as protective as America's now defend South Africans against official abuse. President Mandela told me with pride how the new Constitutional Court, where Chaskalson now presides, had overturned as unconstitutional his proclamation of elections in the Western Cape: "Arthur Chaskalson defended me when I was sent to Robben Island for 27 years. But when it came to the question whether I was entitled to issue those proclamations, he felt I had no right. And he overrode me. And within an hour of his ruling I came out and made a public statement to say this is the highest tribunal in constitutional matters, they handled a complicated case with great skill, and I called upon members of the A.N.C. and the public to respect the decision. I had to do so. It was a fitting opportunity for us to assert the independence of the structures we have put up to show that the Bill of Rights is a living document."

Neville Alexander, Mandela's Marxist fellow prisoner, said: "I don't think his South Africa is going to do much for the people in economic and social terms. But the crucial point of agreement is on a human rights culture."

For me, South Africa remains the most moving, the most exhilarating of countries: a land of possibility. Nelson Mandela made it that, made it a country whose people feel like proud citizens rather than pariahs. And that is not just a product of the transitional years after 1990. It could all have been lost when it came time to form and run a government. Whatever the faults of the Mandela Government—and the critics have a case—the transformation of South Africa into a free and rights-oriented society has been secured. The critics, most of them, recognize that. Richard Steyn, former editor of *The Star*, said: "Mandela is so intent on reconciliation that governing takes second place. We need some tough decisions. But just think where we were!"

"The same leaders who were
champions in the struggle for
freedom and democracy during
colonial and apartheid times have
turned into monsters and autocrats."

SOUTH AFRICA'S POST-APARTHEID GOVERNMENT DOES NOT PROTECT HUMAN RIGHTS

Newton Kanhema

Newton Kanhema is an award-winning journalist for the *Sunday Independent* newspaper in Johannesburg, South Africa. A citizen of Zimbabwe who had resided in South Africa since 1991, Kanhema was visiting the United States in 1997 when the South African government announced that it would bar him from returning there. In the following viewpoint, Kanhema argues that his expulsion was politically motivated because of his critical articles about South Africa's government under President Nelson Mandela. His deportation is but one example of how the government is harassing journalists and in other ways violating political and civil rights—making it similar to other African governments whose leaders ignore human rights with impunity, he concludes.

As you read, consider the following questions:

1. How have the views of African National Congress leaders on democracy changed since they became part of the government, according to Kanhema?
2. How, in the author's view, have journalists been criticized and harassed in South Africa and other African nations?
3. What are the ethical obligations of journalists in Africa, according to the author?

Excerpted from Newton Kanhema, "Africa's 'Journalist of the Year' Suffers a South African Nightmare," *The Harvard International Journal of Press/Politics*, vol. 3, no. 4 (Fall 1998), pp. 126–30. Copyright ©1998 by the President and Fellows of Harvard College and the Massachusetts Institute of Technology.

Some days I pinch myself just to check whether I am sleeping or having a nightmare. Yes, I am being deported and banned from entering South Africa. But I refuse to accept that the "new" South Africa, the Nelson Mandela government, could be blatantly violating my rights, guaranteed in the South African constitution.

Had I been in Nigeria, in Zaire, in Zimbabwe, or in Uganda under Idi Amin, then I would accept this fate without surprise. But it is the "new" South Africa that victimizes me because of the articles I have written, that brands me a prohibited immigrant. The authorities have officially declared that I will not be "allowed to enter the country with or without valid return visa." This action demonstrates that my deportation is politically motivated.

It is painfully hard to be the first reporter banished by Nelson Mandela, symbol of South African freedom, but I do not regret remaining true to my training and my profession. As the South African transition to democracy gains momentum, the simplistic struggle between black and white wanes, and new frontiers emerge.

CHANGES IN SOUTHERN AFRICA

This phenomenon is not peculiar to South Africa. The practice of covering politics within the southern African region has been transformed as the politics of the region have changed. There is relative peace within southern Africa. It has emerged as the most promising and most stable African economic bloc—the Southern African Development Community (SADC). The guns of the independence wars have fallen silent, but the region is struggling to come to terms with itself.

Prisoners, exiles, refugees, guerrilla soldiers, and antiapartheid activists take charge of the reins of government. Apartheid gurus who ruled South Africa with an iron fist go through a metamorphosis into opposition leaders. The media in South Africa are also going through their own changes. Before liberation, it was impossible for a newspaper, let alone a reporter, not to be identified with one side of the conflict. Politicians on both sides had grown to identify media organizations as either for or against their political parties.

After liberation, the African National Congress (ANC) politicians, who had been in the opposition all their lives, found themselves running the government and therefore targets of media scrutiny. Investigations resulted in exposés about scandal and corruption. For those who had stood for universal suffrage and democracy, this has turned into a conspiracy against their hard-won "revolution." While in exile, they could be secretive and not answer to anyone, but now the press and the public are holding them accountable.

"Why do you guys demand transparency from the ANC, and yet you never asked for this from the Nationalist [apartheid] government? Wait until President Mandela goes. We will teach you a lesson," said one senior ANC leader when I spoke to him about my deportation. Before I was deported, President Mandela and his heir apparent, Thabo Mbeki, had taken turns swinging at the press, which they called "antirevolutionary" and "unpatriotic."

ANC politicians are veterans of the war of liberation. When called to answer for misconduct, they question the reporter, "What role did you play in the liberation of the country?" If that does not exonerate them, they remind either their constituency or whoever is listening of the role they played in liberating the "masses."

The mainstream media remain predominantly white, a legacy of apartheid. So Mandela's government attacks the press corps, accusing the media of wishing for a return to the good old days of apartheid. Independent black journalists have been labeled puppets of their "white conservative editors." Recently, Mandela said that black journalists who criticize the government's performance do so to secure promotion. The champions of democracy and freedom of expression during the liberation struggle have turned into champions of ridiculing the media.

In the last three decades, the entire southern African region was engulfed in conflict. That conflict arose out of the remnants of colonialism and the struggle for independence by the black majority. This background seems to have dictated political definitions and directions. The enemy was conspicuous during the time of apartheid: It was anything associated with white superiority or any system that promoted this notion. But today, institutions and individuals have to be careful not to be identified with the past if they stand up against practices contrary to good governance.

POLITICIANS AND JOURNALISTS

In my reporting assignments, I have traveled extensively within southern and central Africa. I have been privileged to meet most of the decision makers from this emerging economic bloc. It would be naive of anyone to believe that the politicians in southern Africa are unique. They believe that they should not be criticized for their poor performance, corruption, and other practices contrary to good governance. Whenever authorities are criticized or called to answer for their actions, they remind their constituencies what it was like during colonialism or apartheid.

As my deportation process continues, there is a debate over whether South Africa has more freedom of expression now than during apartheid. There is no question that today's press is much freer than that of the apartheid era. But this does not mean that the media should turn a blind eye to incidents of intimidation and denials of freedom of expression.

When a journalist exposes the evils of the day, the common reaction from politicians is, "He has a hidden agenda," "He is working for the CIA," "He is a member of some foreign intelligence," or, lately, "He is unpatriotic and a counterrevolutionary." All these inciting labels are meant to mobilize the common people against the journalist in question.

CONTROVERSIAL ARTICLES

My articles have landed me in big trouble, but on the other hand, they have left me with the continent's most prestigious journalism award—African Journalist of the Year.

One article grew out of my fascination with the arms trade. South Africa is a big arms manufacturer. The apartheid government supplied weapons to rogue governments that used them in civil wars like the Rwandan genocide. During an investigation into financial irregularities within a government-owned arms manufacturer, Denel, I stumbled upon information of a proposed $1.5 billion sale to Saudi Arabia and decided to pursue the story.

Authorities first denied the story, then applied for an urgent interdict to stop publication. In the process, they gagged my newspaper, The Sunday Independent. My editor, John Battersby, determined to print, published the article without naming Saudi Arabia. This resulted in an immediate indictment against me and three of the newspapers that had published my article. But the authorities had used the 1968 Official Secrecy Act, with which the present government is not prepared to be associated. Charges against me and the newspapers were withdrawn.

The article was later published with Saudi Arabia identified. But the government spoke of my article's possibly causing the loss of thirty thousand jobs if the arms deal were not signed. As I investigated the story further, I found that the sensitivity emanated from "commissions"—bribes—to high-ranking government officials. The story is not over yet. The bribes could total $120 million.

In 1996 the most popular ANC leader and a former homeland leader, Bantu Holomisa, was expelled from the party because he dared to tell the Truth and Reconciliation Commission that one of Mandela's cabinet members received a $2 million bribe from a casino king. But before the expulsion could be executed, the former homeland leader Bantu Holomisa disclosed that the same casino magnate had given Nelson Mandela an amount equivalent to $500,000 before the election. Although there were denials, I was one of the first reporters to crack the story.

SOUTH AFRICA IS BECOMING A ONE-PARTY STATE

However delightful and heroic a man [Nelson] Mandela is, and no matter how utterly justified his movement's struggle has been, this should not blind one to the fact that the African nationalist party that rules South Africa today is recognizably kin to the similar parties that set up single-party or one-party dominant regimes all over Africa, and that its hegemonic ambitions overlap all too comfortably with the instinctive practices of the old-style Communist Party, which has historically always constituted "the central nervous system" of the African National Congress (ANC).

Although the ANC claims to be democratic, its own internal practices suggest that this is only partially true. Enormous pressure is exerted to ensure that, whenever possible, there is only one candidate for each senior position in the party. Party discipline is extremely strong and is prized above all else. . . .

Above all, the party—it prefers to call itself a liberation movement—is at best ambivalent about the need for opposition parties.

R.W. Johnson, *The National Interest*, Fall 1998.

I also exposed the financial situation of the party—$8 million in the red. Trunks containing millions of dollars donated by Malaysians never arrived at ANC coffers; some of the money ended up in private individuals' trust accounts.

After the Zairian dictator, Mobutu Sese Seko, fled the country in 1997, his generals escaped to South Africa with loot. Their presence in South Africa was a source of diplomatic embarrassment because of the involvement of South African intelligence and high officials in the loot. . . .

I had never felt so happy and so honored as when I was called to the podium to receive the "African Journalist of the Year" award. Usually, this honor calls only for celebration, but my celebration comes with frustration and sadness as an African. I face deportation because of my articles. Deportation would prevent me from carrying on with my life normally. It would remove me from an African country I chose as my home. It would end my career in South Africa.

AFRICAN LEADERS VIOLATE HUMAN RIGHTS

Throughout Africa, wherever human rights were violated, those who spent their lives fighting for freedom are the ones who are robbing their citizens of the freedom for which they were at one time willing to die.

As independence sweeps slowly down the continent, one wonders: Are people in all of these countries free to have an opinion different from that of their leaders? Are citizens of Africa free to express their opinion in public without risking the consequences of banishment, imprisonment, or assassination? It was the white minority who represented the system we all wanted defeated. But today, as citizens and as journalists, we are struggling to suppress our true and genuine disappointment in our own governments. Those governments have done little for the past thirty years to improve the lives of those who put them in power.

We, as journalists, are also afraid to be labeled traitorous, unpatriotic counterrevolutionaries when we dare stand up and say no to actions and programs that deceive and rob the very people our politicians purport to represent. We are possibly the last hope for the African people who gave their children's lives and their own lives to liberate every citizen on the continent. The same leaders who were champions in the struggle for freedom and democracy during colonial and apartheid times have turned into monsters and autocrats. They appear to believe that all of the lives lost during the struggle were lost for their individual freedom and not for universal freedom.

Some journalists are prostituting their ethics to seek popularity with the people who are robbing the society of all of its freedoms. I now wonder: Is it better to be popular with politicians or to serve the public as expected? To serve the profession with honor? To uphold our ethics for the good of democracy and individual human rights? We all know how undemocratic our leaders are, those who continue to blame their failures on the legacy of colonialism, racism, and other evils.

I am tired of African leaders who rape their economies for decades and still heap blame on others. Was it not crazy for a dictator like Mobutu to die blaming the western world for the pathetic nonexistence of the Zairian economy? My own experience with African politicians is that they blame their failure not on themselves, but on whites. And this I have refused to accept. It is time African leaders accept their responsibilities. Those aspiring to higher standards in African journalism have to choose whom they want to be in bed with: the rogue politicians or the victims of those politicians.

I made my choice, and I have met with the consequences. But in every struggle, including this one of freedom of expression, someone has to pay. Those who pay rarely choose to do so. But they pay—I pay—anyway.

PERIODICAL BIBLIOGRAPHY

The following articles have been selected to supplement the diverse views presented in this chapter. Addresses are provided for periodicals not indexed in the *Readers' Guide to Periodical Literature*, the *Alternative Press Index*, the *Social Sciences Index*, or the *Index to Legal Periodicals and Books*.

Lahouari Addi	"Algeria's Army, Algeria's Agony," *Foreign Affairs*, July/August 1998.
Florence Aubenas	"Algeria's 'Disappeared,'" *World Press Review*, April 1998.
Fergus M. Bordewich	"Radical Islam's Bloody Battlefield," *Reader's Digest*, November 1997.
Tania Cordoba	"Diapers and Dictators," *New Internationalist*, January/February 1998.
Anaga Dalal	"Salima Ghezali," *Ms.*, January/February 1998.
Audrey Edwards	"South Africa Reborn," *Essence*, October 1997.
Russ Feingold	"Human Rights: Crucial to U.S. Foreign Policy," *Christian Science Monitor*, February 11, 1998.
Antoinette Handley and Jeffrey Herbst	"South Africa: The Perils of Normalcy," *Current History*, May 1997.
Julius O. Ihonvbere	"Democratization in Africa," *Peace Review*, September 1997.
R.W. Johnson	"Destroying South Africa's Democracy," *National Interest*, Fall 1998.
Stefan Lovgren	"It Takes a Dictatorship to Raise a Democracy," *U.S. News & World Report*, March 23, 1998.
John Mukum Mbaku	"Constitutional Engineering and the Transition to Democracy in Post–Cold War Africa," *Independent Review*, Spring 1998. Available from 100 Swan Wy., Oakland, CA 94621-1428.
Robert Mortimer	"Algeria: The Dialectic of Elections and Violence," *Current History*, May 1997.
J. Oloka-Onyango	"Uganda's 'Benevolent' Dictatorship," *Current History*, May 1997.
Ken Owen	"The Truth Hurts," *New Republic*, November 23, 1998.
David R. Penna and Patricia J. Campbell	"Human Rights and Culture: Beyond Universality and Relativism," *Third World Quarterly*, March 1998.

CHAPTER 4

HOW SHOULD AFRICA'S WILDLIFE BE MANAGED?

CHAPTER PREFACE

One of Africa's noted attributes—and an underpinning of the continent's tourism industry—is its abundant wildlife. African wildlife faces significant threats to its future, however, two of which are habitat encroachment and poaching. Africa's rapidly growing human population increasingly competes with wildlife for resources and land. Meanwhile illegal hunters kill animals for food or for valuable trade commodities. Most noted by the media was the plight of the African elephant. During the 1970s and 1980s poachers killed an estimated seventy thousand specimens annually for their ivory tusks.

African nations and the world community have taken several steps to respond to the twin threats of habitat encroachment and poaching. To protect habitat, Africa has designated 185,000 square miles of land as wildlife reserves and national parks. To protect elephants, the Convention on the International Trade in Endangered Species (CITES) voted in 1989 to enact a total ban on the international ivory trade. This ban has been credited for stopping poaching almost overnight and enabling elephant populations to stabilize, and, in some countries, grow.

However, both the establishing of national parks and the ivory ban have come under criticism for not taking the needs of Africa's people into account. Parks as they exist are seen by some to be relics of colonialism—areas kept off limits to local African populations for the benefit of foreign visitors. Furthermore, the legally protected animals within these sanctuaries frequently leave park boundaries, often trampling crops, consuming food supplies, and endangering humans in the process. Many Africans view these wild animals not as treasured resources, but rather as unwelcome pests. The ban on ivory has also been criticized as an outside imposition on African nations that prevents them from utilizing what would otherwise be a valuable trade resource. The key for future environmental preservation, many argue, is to make it economically rewarding to those who live with wildlife. To this end, many advocate programs that permit controlled hunting of elephants and other animals, the limited selling of ivory tusks, and other activities that may disturb Western environmentalists but provide benefits to African people. Kevin Leo-Smith, an official of Conservation Corporation, a South African ecotourism company, argues that "animals will survive in Africa only if they can produce value to people." The viewpoints in this chapter debate whether such economic considerations should predominate in setting wildlife management policies.

> "Our wild country is terribly vulnerable, protected by a thin membrane . . . that can be torn . . . by the very people who are charged to look after it."

AFRICA'S WILDERNESS MUST BE PRESERVED

Ian Player

Ian Player is director of the Wilderness Foundation, a South African–based preservationist organization. He was for many years a wildlife conservation officer and wilderness guide. In the following viewpoint, taken from a speech given at the Royal Geographical Society in London, he argues that African wildlife areas have scientific, cultural, and spiritual value for both African and non-African peoples, and that special efforts must be made to preserve Africa's remaining wildernesses. Citing the influence of Qumbu Magqubu Ntombela, a Zulu friend, Player describes how he learned to appreciate and live in harmony with nature.

As you read, consider the following questions:

1. What personal experiences in the African wilderness does Player recount?
2. What special significance can African wilderness have for foreign travelers, according to the author?
3. What can the "Western world" do to make up for past colonial exploitations of Africa, according to Player?

Excerpted from Ian Player, "In Defence of Wilderness," *Resurgence*, November/December 1997. Reprinted with permission.

All native peoples had places that were sacred: the Celts and their nemetons, the Ancient Greeks and their forests, the Africans, the native Americans, the Aborigines, all had sacred sites in wilderness that were looked after by the spirits and revered by people.

I must emphasize that there is a very big difference between a national park or a game reserve and a wilderness area. One can have a wilderness area within a park, but of wilderness someone once said, "It is where the moderns at least see what their ancestors knew in their nerves and their blood."

There are many values of wilderness: scientific, historical, educational, recreational and spiritual. . . .

Wilderness is both a geographical area and a philosophical idea. Magqubu Ntombela, my Zulu mentor, was a speaker at the first World Wilderness Congress, which was held in South Africa. Although he could not speak English and had to have an interpreter, he had his audience entranced when he spoke about the seasons of the year. It was quite clear that what modern people regard as wilderness the indigenous people saw as home.

WILDERNESS EXPERIENCES

I went to the Second World War at the age of seventeen. During the war I made a promise to myself to canoe from the city of Pietermaritzburg to the port of Durban, down the rivers that rise in the great Drakensberg mountains of KwaZulu-Natal.

This was my first experience of wilderness. The two rivers run through the Valley of a Thousand Hills. Day after day I paddled alone in deep gorges, sometimes caught in thunder and lightning storms that swept up the rivers. It took seven days to canoe the 110 miles and I entered a new world, and the beginning of an understanding of my relationship to the Earth. But one thing shocked me: I saw very few wild animals; in fact, only two grey duiker. That made me determined to try to do something about wildlife conservation.

I joined the Natal Parks Board in 1952 and served in all the game reserves of Zululand. Lake St. Lucia was my first station. In April and May, the pelicans arrive to breed and at the same time the great mullet shoals gather in their thousands, before moving down the lake on their journey to the sea. Sometimes when the crocodile went in amongst them at night the roar of the fish jumping would wake me. If you shone a light from a boat, so many mullet would jump into it that the boat could sink. My foot patrols took me over the dune forests to the beaches and the great bat caves. I fished for my own food and slept next to driftwood fires. Slowly the wilderness world was weaving its web over me.

HUMAN POWER AND DESTRUCTION

Then I was posted to Ndumu game reserve on the Mozambique border, some of the wildest country left in South Africa. A friend sent me Laurens van der Post's book, *Venture to the Interior*. It made me aware that we, the Caucasians, had not acknowledged the noble soul of Africa. In fact, we attacked it in every possible technological way. We killed the people we called "the savages". My own great-grandfather was in the colonial army and was sent to shoot Bushpeople. The only thing that remains today of the Bushpeople in the Drakensberg mountains is a hundred miles of caves with their exquisite paintings. Sometimes I sit in them in the late afternoon and the evening, and in my imagination I can hear the Bushpeople talking. The paintings glow numinously, but the morning light shows the obscenities written by our own people on and above these wonderful works of art. You have to ask who is civilized?

Africa has always been regarded as a poor relation by the rest of the world. But Africa has made contributions that few people have taken time to think about.

The old Africa is almost gone. My work as a game ranger made me realize that humankind has a terrible power and is systematically wiping out species, destroying ecosystems and eliminating wilderness.

A ZULU MENTOR

My own understanding of the mysteries of Africa came through Qumbu Magqubu Ntombela, a Zulu, who led me along the rhino, hippo and elephant trails in Mfolozi game reserve. These were the old hunting grounds of the early Zulu kings. I began to see the country through his eyes and learn how his culture had valued it. I learnt to appreciate how they respected the animals. Even when they killed them, they did so with deep respect because they said that every animal had a spirit and you had to acknowledge it. . . .

I grew to appreciate that this was a very great man. He became my leader, teacher and mentor.

He taught me the need to respect the whole natural world. He began by telling me the Zulu months of the year. Each Zulu name describes the changing season. April is the first nip of cold and people start making fires in their huts, and June is when the trees start to shed their leaves. July is the beginning of the wind

160

that blows the leaves off the trees and the world is full of dust. In October the paths are covered by grass that has started to grow after the first rains. November is when the pumpkins become ripe and in December the wildebeest give birth to their calves.

I knew then that what Henry Miller had said was true: "The world is not to be put in order, the world is order incarnate. It is for us to put ourselves in unison with this order to know what is world order." In my forty-four years with Magqubu Ntombela I learned to know that he was in harmony with that world.

WILDERNESS AND RECREATION

What remains of African wilderness is of the greatest importance because Africa can provide recreation in the true meaning of the word. To re-create something inside ourselves. This will give us the opportunity to build a stronger symbiotic relationship between Africa and the Western world. Africa can help the world, particularly spiritually. Amongst many people in the West there is a weariness caused by travel without a purpose. Instead of the pilgrimages we once went on, we travel to escape. Africa can reintroduce the tradition of pilgrimage and bring a new dimension to travel. To sleep beside lonely fires on the red earth in the African bush will connect us to a primeval part of ourselves.

ESTABLISHING PRIORITIES

Boundaries [of national parks and reserves] must be kept intact and protected. We need to recognise that national parks are sacrosanct; they are not larders to be plundered . . . and exploited by later corrupt governments.

We must get our priorities right: nature is invaluable. Biodiversity cannot be given a price. We must stop messing about with it from a sense of guilt.

It is unrealistic to think we will go forward by saying that species must pay to stay, given Africa's present constructs. It is homo sapiens who must pay. The point is that species must stay, so we must pay.

Richard Leakey, quoted in the *Electronic Mail & Guardian*, October 1, 1997.

In African wilderness there is an ancient spirit, said to be older than the human spirit. And it still survives in the vast, brooding acacia bushveld, in some of the remote mountains and along the wild coastlines. What we have in these wild lands are the most precious of our worldly gifts. But our wild country is terribly vulnerable, protected by a thin membrane, a caul that can be torn and rendered useless, frequently by the very people who are charged to look after it.

In my life I have tried to make allies and win over people to help us in this great battle for wild Africa. I was fortunate in my time to have wilderness areas set aside in Zululand. I have worked for forty years as a wildlife conservation officer and as a director with non-governmental wilderness organizations. Magqubu and I took over 1,000 people on wilderness treks. I wanted to make people appreciate the wilderness. I wanted them to be touched by the small remaining wild landscapes of Zululand. But without Magqubu Ntombela this would never have been possible. He was the inspiration, the teacher and the interpreter of the African land. . . .

Africa is a huge continent and many of the countries within it are in a convulsive uproar. It is, I believe, at its own pace slowly re-establishing its ancient pattern, and if the Western world could re-enforce the protection of real wilderness areas, this would be the best recompense for the colonial exploitations of the past.

> "Management strategies must make
> conservation profitable for rural
> communities that border on Africa's
> remaining natural areas."

AFRICA'S WILDERNESS SHOULD BE COMMERCIALLY UTILIZED TO BENEFIT LOCAL COMMUNITIES

Henri Nsanjama

Africa leads the world in setting land aside for wilderness protection, argues Henri Nsanjama in the following viewpoint. However, Africa's rapidly growing human population will place growing pressure on its wildlife. Nsanjama contends that African nations must link environmental protection with economic development for Africa's poor. By developing tourism and related businesses, local communities that border national parks and preservation areas should be able to derive direct economic benefits from conservation efforts. The closing off of national parks entirely from local populations—a practice begun when Africa was under European colonial rule—must be rethought, he concludes. Nsanjama is vice president of the African and Madagascar Program of the World Wildlife Fund (WWF), an international conservation organization.

As you read, consider the following questions:

1. When were national parks first created in Africa, according to Nsanjama?
2. What does the author say is the greatest threat to endangered species in Africa?
3. According to Nsanjama, what conservation traditions existed in Africa prior to European contact?

Reprinted from Henri Nsanjama, "People and Animals Vie for Africa's Ecosystems," *Forum for Applied Research and Public Policy*, Summer 1997, with permission.

The African continent comprises tremendous cultural wealth and diversity. In fact, more than 500 million people representing more than 1,500 ethnic groups and speaking as many languages and dialects inhabit the continent.

Africa's natural environment boasts a similarly rich diversity of ecosystems, ranging from the remote and arid Kalahari Desert of East Namibia and Botswana in southern Africa to the 19,000-foot snow-capped summit of Mount Kilimanjaro situated in the populous region of Tanzania in east central Africa.

Then there are the complex and beautiful coral reefs of Madagascar off the southeast coast of Africa; the nearby islands of Mauritius, Seychelles, and Zanzibar set in the Indian Ocean; and the dry forests and savannas of eastern and southern Africa, home to some of the world's largest animals. The continent's lush rain forests stretch from Guinea on the western coast inland to Zaire in central Africa.

These diverse ecosystems provide habitat for some of the world's more conspicuous—and in some cases, largest—animals, including elephants, zebras, giraffes, rhinos, and lions.

The people of Africa have learned to value this wealth of diversity, and today, Africa leads the world in setting aside lands for wildlife conservation.

In fact, in some countries, among them Tanzania, national parks cover more than 10 percent of the land mass. The percentage increases to 25 percent when Tanzania's forest reserves are added.

CONSERVATION IN AFRICA

National parks were first created in Africa under edicts passed by European colonial powers beginning in 1925. Following the decline of colonialism in Africa in the post-World War II era, most national governments continued to maintain—and in many cases expanded—their networks of national parks and protected habitats.

Increased emphasis on protection of these natural ecosystems and their resident species has proven both a blessing and a curse to the people of Africa.

On the one hand, the reserves have ensured the survival of species and ecosystems that might have otherwise been eradicated.

On the other hand, the reserves have frayed the historic relationship between the people of Africa and the continent's natural systems, a relationship that has helped sustain African culture for centuries. In many cases, local inhabitants are forbidden from even setting foot inside national parks without a permit.

Further complicating the issue is that the population of Africa likely will double within the next 25 years. As the number of people in Africa surges upward, overcrowding—particularly in the continent's urban areas—will increase.

As a result, governments across the continent will face rising pressure to develop some of the lands currently protected as parks.

The growth of Nairobi, Kenya, for example, has had a devastating impact on Nairobi National Park; similarly, the growth of Lusaka, Zambia, has placed nearby Lochinvar National Park at risk.

MEANS AND ENDS

In view of these developments, many naturalists have begun to recognize that a complete "hands-off" approach to conservation—that is, entirely closing national parks to use by indigenous peoples—may no longer be feasible.

Indeed, it appears that the only viable option facing African governments is to find a way to link conservation efforts to human needs, particularly the needs of the rural poor. As we have learned in the past, villagers, deprived of the means for making a legal living wage, may turn to poaching and other crimes that ultimately threaten the health of large protected areas.

Such activities as ecotourism within national parks and trophy hunting in selected areas would provide employment opportunities for the rural poor and offer the greatest potential for sharing the bounty of Africa's resources among all its people.

Any provisions to allow hunting must, of course, be managed in a way that ensures the survival of at-risk species. Though this goal sounds simple, it may prove difficult to achieve because Africa's reserves cover a vast area, and hunting restrictions would be difficult to enforce.

It's useful to note, however, that the wanton slaughter of wild animals for commercial trade poses only a modest risk to the long-term survival of target species.

The greatest threat to these species, in fact, is the impending conflict between people and animals for a finite amount of living space. As humans develop more and more arable land, ecosystems become fragmented and animals, deprived of resources—and space necessary for survival—often die.

In such small countries as Lesotho and Swaziland, both of which are completely surrounded by South Africa, the struggle for space was resolved long ago to the detriment of many large species, among them elephants. Humans were permitted to develop the land, and elephants were forced to migrate to remaining wild regions or perished.

LOSING HABITAT

The most widely understood threat to the African wildlife survival is poaching for commercial trade in elephant tusks, rhino horns, and the pelts of leopards and other exotic species.

Western animal-welfare groups have responded to this threat by championing the cause of a number of endangered species, including elephants, rhinos, and gorillas. Print and broadcast media worldwide have enthusiastically supported such efforts.

Though this heartfelt support has been valuable in calling attention to specific endangered species, it fails to recognize the over-arching threat to species survival in Africa, which is habitat loss.

ENDANGERED SPECIES AND PRIVATE OWNERSHIP

Over the years the benefits of private ownership and cooperative conservancies have accrued to a range of endangered species. Liberal game ranching laws now accommodate the lucrative business of crocodile farming. Crocodile eggs are collected in the wild, and the hatchlings are raised for domestic slaughter. A significant percentage, though, are returned to the wild to seed new populations. Once on the edge of extinction, crocodiles are now thriving in areas of Southern Africa where their commercial exploitation is allowed.

The benefits of private enterprise have also spilled over to non-farmed wildlife. Black and white rhinos, for example, are flourishing on private ranches, and elephants are making dramatic comebacks. More telling still is the tale and status of leopards and cheetahs, species long viewed and treated as vermin by ranchers fearful for the well-being of their livestock. In Zimbabwe, leopards were removed from protected status, endowing them with high market value as trophies and pelts. Now that leopards are money-making assets, their numbers are on the up-swing, and the use of dogs or traps to gratuitously kill them is blocked by social sanction and the economic incentive to sustain a flourishing population for lucrative hunts. In contrast, cheetahs, which were less numerous than leopards, were kept in protected status, suppressing whatever commercial value they might have had. They remain, for that reason, imperiled; they are, in ranchers' eyes, vermin with no redeeming value.

Karl Hess Jr., *Reason*, October 1997.

The assumption that wildlife populations will be out of danger once poaching stops is both dangerous and naive. This assumption also might serve to undermine international conservation efforts. Even in areas where poaching has been brought under control, habitat destruction remains a severe threat.

Ironically, the threat also works in reverse. That is, in some cases, encroachment of animals from national parks into developed areas can adversely affect human settlements.

For example, animals—particularly large ones—pose a threat to crop lands. Indeed, elephants, which have no regard for human landmarks or property rights, can stray beyond the confines of a reserve and cause severe damage, not only to subsistence crops, but to cash crops—among them tea, coffee, and cotton.

It's possible for an African village to lose an entire year's crop as well as its stored harvests and seed grains in a single night to a herd of elephants.

When the problem reaches this level, all intellectual issues of global biological diversity have no meaning, particularly for Africa's subsistence farmers for whom a field of corn can spell the difference between survival and starvation.

BALANCING INTERESTS

The key to successful conservation of African wildlife and the continent's park system lies in the sustainable management of the resource itself. Such a management approach must take into account the widest scope of needs and interests.

Specifically, management strategies must make conservation profitable for rural communities that border on Africa's remaining natural areas.

In other words, these rural communities must derive direct economic benefits from conservation and resource management through ecotourism, hunting fees, and the sale of food, crafts, medicinal products, and other goods and services that appeal to consumers worldwide.

Local communities will pledge their support for maintaining large wildlife areas as parks only if they can be convinced of the economic benefits of keeping parcels of land under natural vegetation.

Such ties between people and the land have been developed in several African nations, including Malawi, Nambia, and Central Africa Republic.

CONSERVING TRADITIONS

Conservation in Africa predates the arrival of European settlers. In fact, centuries before the Europeans arrived, African leaders set aside parcels of land for conservation for the exclusive use of royal families and other elite members of society. Land also was set aside for traditional and cultural festivals.

Though conservation is not new to Africa, many of the threats that now imperil both the national parks and their native inhabitants are.

Until these problems are addressed in a way that ensures the survival of both humans and animal species, they will devour more resources by the day.

| "Controlled safari hunting . . . must be recognized as a legitimate form of ecotourism."

COMMERCIAL HUNTING OF WILDLIFE CAN BE BENEFICIAL

CAMPFIRE Association and the Africa Resources Trust

In 1989 the southern African nation of Zimbabwe began the Communal Areas Management Program for Indigenous Resources (CAMPFIRE). Under this program and similar ones established in other nations, local residents of communal lands surrounding national parks and wildlife preserves are encouraged to utilize wildlife as an economic resource. Much of the money that is earned through CAMPFIRE and redistributed to local communities comes from selling hunting licenses to European and American trophy hunters. In the following viewpoint, two groups who collaborate in administering CAMPFIRE—the CAMPFIRE Association and the Africa Resources Trust—argue that hunting is an important component of the sustainable management of African wildlife. Giving local residents an economic stake in wildlife reduces illegal poaching while providing resources for schools, medical clinics, and other community projects.

As you read, consider the following questions:

1. What has been the traditional relationship between rural Africans and wild animals, according to the authors?
2. Why do trophy hunters cause less damage to the environment than other tourists, according to the authors?
3. How have CAMPFIRE programs changed the views of many rural Africans towards wildlife?

Reprinted, with permission, from "Hunting: Funding Rural Development and Wildlife Conservation in CAMPFIRE," Factsheet #12 of the CAMPFIRE Association and the Africa Resources Trust.

For thousands of years, rural Africans have relied on plentiful supplies of impala and other game animals for meat, clothing and income. Ironically, rural Zimbabweans have recently begun laying down their spears and bows, whilst at the same time encouraging foreign hunters to hunt elephants, buffaloes, lions or other wild animals on their lands. The reason is a simple matter of economics—foreign sport hunters will pay large sums to hunt Africa's trophy animals, far more than other tourists will pay to view them. A single hunter can spend more than US $40,000 on a trophy hunting trip. Under the CAMPFIRE programme, at least half of that revenue goes to the local communities for rural development and environmental conservation.

At the moment, CAMPFIRE depends on hunting revenues which contribute over 90% of total income to the districts and communities participating in the programme. In 1993, twelve districts participating in CAMPFIRE, with a human population of nearly 400,000 people, earned US $1,516,693 from trophy fees. This is a small sum per individual on average, but some resource rich areas earn disproportionate amounts and even small sums of cash can create meaningful infrastructure when well invested.

HUNTING IS LOW-IMPACT TOURISM

Many communal lands in Zimbabwe lack tourist infrastructure and are unsuitable for photographic tourism. A combination of low game population density and thick bush often means that it is hard to get good sightings of wildlife. However, wealthy people (predominantly from the USA, Germany and Spain) are keen to hunt there to help communities.

Trophy hunters have a much lower impact on the environment than other tourists. They consume a much smaller proportion of resources (such as water), are happy with the most basic infrastructure, and tend to travel in small numbers. All foreign sportsmen have to be accompanied by a licensed professional hunter, who acts as a guide and is trained in wildlife management and skilled at tracking and hunting with minimum disturbance to the wildlife and its habitat. A national parks game scout accompanies hunters to ensure that quotas are observed, and hunting is banned between dusk and dawn.

Every year local communities—with the technical assistance of the Department of National Parks, the World Wildlife Fund (WWF) and other organisations—conduct a census of wildlife and determine a sustainable quota of animals that can be hunted on their lands that season. The quotas also allow for Problem Animal Control—the culling of individual animals which are persistent pests to people, their livestock or crops. Quotas ensure that wildlife populations are maintained at a level suitable for the local environment.

'Our people have stopped poaching. They understand that a buffalo is worth much more if it is killed by a foreign hunter.' Champion Machaya, Dete wildlife committee

CHANGING ATTITUDES ON WILDLIFE CONSERVATION

For most rural Africans wildlife is a nuisance, posing a serious threat to their livelihoods and sometimes their lives. Lions and leopards prey on their livestock, and elephants and buffalo trample their crops, often destroying the people's only source of subsistence and income in the process. Until now, the only solution has been to illegally 'poach' animals for their meat, or to call for the Department of National Parks to cull individual problem animals. However, given a steady income from trophy hunting, rural people are now motivated to conserve and manage their wildlife, and have the funds to protect their villages and crops.

Through CAMPFIRE, hunting contributes to environmental conservation in Zimbabwe's communal areas. For example:

• Young people from each CAMPFIRE area are trained to be game scouts to prevent poaching and assist in local wildlife management.

• Revenues from hunting are used by CAMPFIRE communities to undertake animal censuses, provide environmental education and prevent poaching.

• Hwange district council has imported wildlife onto communal lands, where the wildlife population had been decimated.

• During drought years, Beitbridge residents have drilled wells to provide water for elephants, and supplied emergency food for wildlife.

• Land is being zoned and set aside for wildlife. For example, the Mahenye community abandoned its villages on Ngwachumeni Island to turn it into a wildlife management area. They have stopped cutting down trees so as to improve wildlife habitat and have also banned grazing of cattle outside their community boundaries, with the objective of increasing the amount of habitat available for wildlife.

'Most of our hunters are keen conservationists, so their aim is not to shoot as many as possible, but to bag a prime specimen. They come to us because they know we can provide the goods, but also because their money is going into supporting conservation.' Bill Bedford, Ingwe Safaris

Through CAMPFIRE, rural communities use funds generated from hunting to assist their development. Elected committees decide how to distribute the funds according to local needs and priorities. During drought years, money tends to be distributed mainly as household incomes. In more abundant years, funds are directed towards community development projects such as building roads and clinics, installing grinding mills and drilling wells.

Reprinted by permission of Chuck Asay and Creators Syndicate.

Masoka village is in the Zambezi Valley, an area teeming with big game. Every year, its residents meet under the mango tree to decide what to do with the money they receive from their hunting concessions. In 1993, they used their hunting profits—some US $56,000—to build a health clinic, buy a tractor, and expand their school. They also agreed to pay the tuition of their 315 school children, and maintain the 12-mile electric fence that protects villagers and their fields from marauding animals. Thanks to hunting, people whose livestock or crops are damaged by wildlife are paid compensation, and funds are used to pay for an anti-poaching unit. In addition, at the end of each successful hunting trip, the meat is distributed free to the community nearest to where the animal was hunted.

MAKING THE MOST OF WILDLIFE RESOURCES
There are several steps that could or should be taken to enable rural communities to make the most of their wildlife resources:

• Wildlife utilisation has to be recognised as a sustainable development tool. The international community must acknowledge that projects aiming for both wildlife conservation and human development can work and are desirable. International legislation should support this, not discriminate against it.

• Similarly, controlled safari hunting—such as that which takes place in Zimbabwe—must be recognised as a legitimate form of ecotourism.

• Research and technical inputs are needed to enable rural communities to maximise hunting revenues in CAMPFIRE areas. For example, a small number of cheaper trophy safaris could be held in the wet season, so that foreign hunters could pay the trophy fees for 'problem animals' which will be culled in any case. Research could be done to investigate the potential for rural communities to host bow hunting, which is the fastest growing sport in the USA. Big game bow hunts are being run by some commercial farmers in Zimbabwe, but it has yet to be tried in CAMPFIRE areas.

| "In wild animal populations lethal utilisation is rarely, if ever, sustainable."

COMMERCIAL HUNTING OF WILDLIFE IS NOT BENEFICIAL

David Barrit

Many communities in South Africa, Zimbabwe, and other African nations rely on hunting as a source of income. Trophy hunters pay thousands of dollars for permission to hunt big game such as elephants. In the following viewpoint, David Barrit criticizes the practice of selling hunting licenses. Not only is it inhumane to kill animals for sport, he argues, but hunting also makes little economic sense. Africans should instead focus on photo safaris and other nonlethal forms of tourism as the best way to utilize and preserve their wildlife resources. Barrit is the African director of the International Fund for Animal Welfare, an animal rights organization.

As you read, consider the following questions:

1. What central issue divides South Africa's conservation movement, according to Barrit?
2. Why does Barrit believe that hunting is not economically sound for South Africa?
3. How much does an elephant earn for a country over the course of its life, according to a Kenyan investigation cited by the author?

Reprinted from David Barrit, "The Case Against Culling," *The Electronic Mail and Guardian,* March 1996, by permission.

A battle is being waged in South Africa for the soul of conservation. On one side are "sustainable users" who say the only way to save animals is to kill them; on the other are those who see animals as sentient beings who should be allowed to live in peace—the animal welfare lobby. The outcome of this battle will decide the fate of South Africa's wildlife far into the future.

At issue is whether South Africa will become a game-viewing destination with a highly developed eco-tourism industry, or a country where animals are viewed as utility creatures to be hunted for trophies and "harvested" for body-parts.

THE FLAWS OF "SUSTAINABLE USE"

"Sustainable users" want the latter. They say by allowing hunting, there will be economic incentives for humans to keep animals around. There are many flaws in this argument, the most fundamental being that in wild animal populations lethal utilisation is rarely, if ever, sustainable.

For example, such a demand was created for ivory in the Seventies that massive poaching almost destroyed East Africa's elephant population. Only a worldwide ban in the international ivory trade saved them.

Cape Fur seals are another example. The Namibian government enshrined the concept of "sustainable utilisation" in the Constitution and sealers take advantage of this to conduct a trade in seal penises for aphrodisiacs. When a natural disaster wiped out hundreds of thousands of seals in 1994, government scientists said there should be no "harvest" for several years.

Yet, faced with demands from sealers, the government permitted tens of thousands of seals to be killed, with potentially dire consequences for the long-term viability of the population.

ECONOMIC BENEFITS OF WILDLIFE PRESERVATION

Quite apart from issues such as these, those who say that killing South Africa's wildlife is the best way to benefit from them economically, are just plain wrong. South Africa can be the most important safari destination in Africa, attracting visitors from all over the world, creating many jobs and earning large amounts of foreign exchange.

South Africa's unique selling point, the thing that will entice visitors to part with hard-earned cash, is our wildlife. Yes, we have a good infrastructure, superb scenery and sunny weather, but there are holiday destinations with all of the above which are cheaper and more easily accessible.

It is the prospect of viewing wildlife which will induce visitors to make lengthy trips to our shores, and yet South Africa has far less land set aside for game reserves than other African countries. To ensure our tourism industry takes off we need many more live animals. The Kruger National Park and the private reserves that adjoin it are close to capacity. We need to develop reserves in other parts of the country with attractions to rival Kruger.

The Habitat of the African Elephant

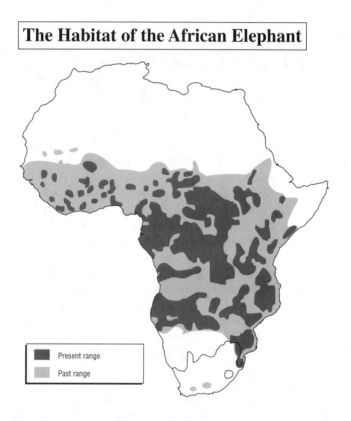

Present range
Past range

We also have to remember the basic truth that when visitors to South Africa go on safari, they want to see lots of animals. This is an important point because some "sustainable users" argue that trophy hunting and photographic safaris can co-exist in game reserves.

Making Animals Shy

The problem is that where hunting exists, animals become shy; they learn to keep out of the way of vehicles and humans. The most effective way of advertising is word-of-mouth; we want tourists to return home and tell their friends that they saw all kinds of animals at close quarters, not that they caught a glimpse of an elephant heading for the horizon.

The same argument applies to trading in animal parts. "Sustainable users" want the ivory trade ban lifted and if that happens we can say goodbye to elephants, for example, as poaching will inevitably follow.

In the past poaching was contained thanks to the army patrolling our border to prevent guerrilla incursions. It was serendipity that our animals were also protected, but we no longer have those patrols. If we create a legal ivory market, an illegal market will flourish with catastrophic consequences.

South Africa's animals are a national treasure of incalculable worth. It may well be, as a Kenyan investigation concluded, that in the course of its life every elephant earns the country R4-million (rand). Even if it were not so, I would argue against hunting as I believe that elephants enrich our lives and that treating them as things to be slaughtered diminishes us as people. For that reason alone, I would argue we should live and let live.

| "Live elephants must remain valuable and ivory must remain valueless to all international markets."

THE BAN ON IVORY TRADE IS NECESSARY TO PROTECT ELEPHANTS

Abdul Shareef

The following viewpoint is taken from a 1996 speech by Abdul Shareef, a diplomat and head of the Tanzanian High Commission to Great Britain. Shareef argues that elephant populations in Tanzania and other African countries plunged during the 1970s and 1980s due to poaching fueled by the ivory trade. Efforts by the Convention on International Trade in Endangered Species (CITES) to partially control the trade did little to stop illegal hunting, he maintains. Only when CITES agreed in 1989 to a flat ban of all international trade in ivory did elephant populations begin to recover. Shareef asserts that any steps to fully or partially reopen the international trade in ivory and other elephant by-products would jeopardize the survival of the animals and threaten Africa's tourism industry.

As you read, consider the following questions:

1. How has the elephant population of Tanzania changed since 1989, according to Shareef?
2. How have elephant poachers reacted to proposals to legalize the ivory trade?
3. What does Shareef list as some of the positive effects of the ivory ban?

Adapted from "How to Save the Elephants: An African Answer to an African Question," a speech delivered by Abdul Shareef to the Environmental Investigation Agency, London, October 17, 1996. Reprinted with permission.

M any of you will vividly recall the disaster which struck the African elephant in the 1970s and 1980s, a disaster of such magnitude that, in May 1989, my government felt it had no choice but to call for a total ban on international trade in elephant products, especially ivory. This meant moving the African elephant from Appendix II to Appendix I of the Convention on International Trade in Endangered Species (CITES). Appendix I is the list of the most endangered species in world trade, and species listed on it may not be traded internationally.

The ban was seen as a last resort. Over a period of many years, the international conservation community had tried all possible means of controlling the ivory trade but it proved too much for anyone to control. For instance, prior to the ban, the African elephant was placed on Appendix II of CITES, but the controls provided by CITES itself were not sufficient to stamp-out illegal ivory trade. Consequently, further control measures, including the establishment of a quota system and an attempt to distinguish raw and worked ivory were imposed by conference resolution at CITES meetings. But with time it became more than obvious that the CITES ivory trade control measures were not working necessitating listing of the African elephant on Appendix I of CITES. Tanzania alone, which had the second largest elephant population in Africa, lost more than 80% of its elephant population. 70 elephants were killed by poachers every day! Hence, my government decision, after extensive consultations and careful examination of all other options, supported the move to upgrade the elephants to Appendix I.

It should not be forgotten that our opponents in the fight to protect elephants were—and still are—ruthless and wealthy international smuggling syndicates, who had developed ever more sophisticated ways of circumventing any regulations which could be devised. For many African governments, resources were scarce and it became pretty clear that if the developed nations which were consumers of ivory could not control the illegal trade in their countries, with all the resources available to them, African governments with far fewer resources did not stand a chance.

THE BAN HAS WORKED

There was disagreement over whether the ban would work or not. I can tell you now, without hesitation, that it did. Poaching dropped to very low levels in many parts of my country, and in some places it stopped altogether. The price of ivory fell to a fraction of what it had been. Poachers no longer had an incentive to risk their lives for ivory that will not sell and scouts and rangers, whose job it is to protect elephants were given a huge morale boost once they realised that they were no longer on the losing side.

At the same time as submitting our proposal for a ban, my government also launched Operation Uhai—A Life Saving Operation—a massive anti-poaching operation which swept virtually the whole country from north to south. Hundreds of poachers were arrested and an enormous amount of ivory, to the tune of more than 50 tonnes, was confiscated. That, combined with the ban, inflicted a mortal wound on the illegal ivory trade in Tanzania, from which, I am pleased to say, it has never recovered. The huge amounts of money used for anti-poaching operations was reduced to less than a quarter of the original costs; and the savings were diverted to other wildlife projects.

Our elephant population is steadily recovering now. In 1989, prior to the ban, the population was reduced to around 50,000 elephants, from 316,000. Today [October 1996] 73,459 elephants roam the country.

Ordinary people all over the world realised that buying ivory meant dead elephants, and consumption of ivory fell precipitously. The markets of Europe and the USA collapsed and in Japan and the Far East, the single largest consumer of ivory, retail sales fell drastically—by 50 to 60%. That is a remarkable achievement.

All this happened seven years ago but we, and our elephants, are still reaping the benefits. Poaching is still low in most areas and the illegal trade is still at far lower levels than before the ban.

DEBATES ON RELAXING THE BAN

The main threat to the stability that we now enjoy is the possibility that the international ivory trade may become legal again. My government believes that the elephants could not withstand the poaching onslaught that would result from such a move, and we are very concerned that the pro-trade lobby is making headway in its campaign to re-open the trade.

Allow me to outline briefly for you what has occurred during this ongoing CITES debate in the seven years since the ban. CITES now has 132 member states, which meet every two years to debate international conservation issues. . . .

The ban came into effect in January 1990. At the 1992 meeting, it was proposed that some five African countries should be allowed to "downlist" their elephants back to Appendix II, to allow resumed sale of elephant products. When it became clear that majority African opinion opposed such a move, the proposal was amended to exclude ivory but to allow the sale of elephant skins and other parts, such as feet. Most African countries still opposed the move, simply because such a move—as experience showed—would trigger once again the poaching onslaught on the elephants, and the proposal was, therefore, withdrawn before it even came to a vote. During this meeting in 1992, east, west and central Africa made a concerted effort to inform the member states of CITES of the danger of reopening the trade.

"IT'S REALLY BETTER THIS WAY. AT THE MOST, I'LL GET MUGGED."

Dave Catrow. Reprinted by permission of Copley News Service.

We had to do the same thing in 1994, when one African state—with some legitimate reasons—proposed downlisting its elephants to Appendix II, with a voluntary moratorium on ivory sales. Notwithstanding the main arguments, we felt, along with so many other African countries, the problem is basically a problem of the whole continent and that the commercialising of any elephant body parts would threaten the success of the ban and the safety of our elephants as a whole; as a result we opposed it. The proposal was withdrawn before a vote, and the official press release cited majority African opposition as the main reason for its withdrawal.

At both these CITES meetings, officials in east Africa stated that they had detected a slight, but very noticeable, increase in elephant poaching in the months immediately prior to CITES, which was attributed to proposals to resume the trade. Once CITES was over, and the ban remained intact, this poaching subsided again. This appears to be a trend not only prior to CITES but also when there is the mere possibility of even having a meeting with the intention of developing a regional position for the next CITES meeting in 1997, in terms of the possible downgrading of elephants to Appendix II. Two weeks ago for instance, my government managed to confiscate, at one go, 20 tonnes of ivory, with every sign that the ivory involved was a result of recent poaching activities. (This to date, brings the total amount of confiscated ivory in government's hands to more than 120 tonnes!)

If the mere possibility of trade causes an upsurge in poaching, we can only dread to think what would happen if legal trade were actually to resume! . . .

ELEPHANTS AND TOURISM

The positive effects of the ban have been manifold. Apart from the reduction in poaching and the gradual recovery of the elephant population, there have been other major benefits. We have begun to help our people to realise the economic potential of live elephants. The elephant is one of the major drawcards in African wildlife tourism and the revenue which can be earned by live elephants, for the benefit of our country as a whole, far outweighs any possible revenue from ivory trade. For instance we discovered that a single live elephant in our National Parks brings in revenue from tourism, within a period of three months only, the equivalent of the price of ivory of 30 dead elephants.

In the past seven years [since 1989], tourism to the United Republic of Tanzania has increased enormously. In 1989, the year of the ban, our tourism receipts amounted to USD [United States dollars] 60 million. In 1995 we earned USD 258 million. We expect to welcome 326,000 visitors to our country in 1996, compared with 138,000 in 1989. We believe the stability of our elephant populations has been a major contributor to this growth. Tourists expect to see peaceful, unstressed wildlife when they visit Tanzania. No tourist wants to see a landscape littered with elephant carcasses and reverberating with the sound of gunfire, and neither do the Tanzanian people. That is why tourism has been dubbed "the peace industry". If the poachers return to their automatic weapons, our wildlife areas will once again become battle fields and that peace will be shattered. Our people and our country will suffer, while international traders in ivory will be quite comfortable in their palaces abroad—totally unconcerned.

The way forward now, I believe, is for those countries with elephant populations to make the most of their wild elephants and to make sure that elephant and people can live together to the mutual benefit of both. Live elephants must remain valuable and ivory must remain valueless to all international markets.

The most important element of the ban—without which it would have been far less successful—was the simple message that it sent to the world: "Come and see live elephants. Come and shoot the elephants, but not with your guns—with your cameras. Don't buy dead ones; buy frozen ones on photographs and books".

My government believes that this is still the message that should be heard around the world, if elephants are to thrive for the benefit of all.

| "The ivory-trade ban effectively
penalizes Zimbabwe for supporting a
healthy population of elephants."

THE BAN ON INTERNATIONAL IVORY TRADE HAS HARMFUL CONSEQUENCES

Wendy Marston

In 1989 an international ban on the trading of ivory was put into place to protect African elephants. Some African nations, including Zimbabwe and Botswana, have since called for a full or partial relaxation of that prohibition. In the following viewpoint, Wendy Marston argues that the ivory trading ban has had unintended harmful consequences. As elephant populations have grown, they have in many places become dangerous pests that inflict extensive environmental and economic damage. She asserts that African nations, such as Zimbabwe, who bear the costs of maintaining healthy elephant populations should be allowed to treat them as a sustainable resource and permit the hunting of elephants and sale of their ivory. Marston, a contributing editor to *Health* magazine, writes about science and the environment.

As you read, consider the following questions:

1. What is Zimbabwe's version of "Fort Knox"?
2. What two visions of wildlife protection are being expressed in the debate over the ivory trade ban, according to Marston?
3. What examples of environmental damage caused by elephants does the author provide?

Reprinted from Wendy Marston, "The Ivory Ban: Good Intentions, Tragic Consequences," *The Washington Post National Weekly Edition*, June 16, 1997, p. 23, by permission.

On the outskirts of the capital city of Zimbabwe, there is a building that some sardonic government officials have dubbed "Fort Knox." Inside, beyond the armed guards and locked doors, sit tons of animal tusks and horns. They might not be worth as much as the gold that the U.S. government used to keep in Fort Knox, Ky., but they are worth millions of dollars—at least potentially.

The shelves of the climate-controlled storeroom are lined with pair after pair of elephant tusks, collected from pachyderms that perished of natural causes or were culled to limit herd size. Each bears the official Zimbabwean stamp of approval. Yet, for now, these treasures are effectively worthless. Because of a ban on ivory trading since 1989, there is no legal market for the elephant tusks, and thus no government revenue.

Zimbabwe, as well as Botswana and Namibia, are pushing to change all that. At the biennial Convention on International Trade in Endangered Species (CITES) of wild flora and fauna, taking place through June 20, 1997, Zimbabwean officials are proposing that elephants be removed from the most endangered category of animal; that the ivory ban be lifted; that Zimbabwe be allowed to sell a shipment of tusks once a year to Japan; that Zimbabwe and other countries also be allowed to export elephant hides; and that they be allowed to trade in live animals, such as selling elephants to zoos. These ideas are sure to be contested sharply.

Two Visions

The question of reopening the ivory trade pits two visions of wildlife conservation against each other: pure protection and sustained utilization. Pure protection seeks to insulate, if not isolate, endangered species from the encroachment of civilization. It regards legalized trading in rare animals or plants as an inherent threat to species survival. Sustained utilization, by contrast, seeks to maintain a healthy population of animals or plants so that they can be hunted or cultivated for profit. Unless wildlife has a dollar value, this approach holds, the people who live around it will have no incentive to protect it.

Although pure protection is morally and theoretically attractive, sustainable utilization has practical advantages that may not be obvious at first glance. Allowing people to make money off of threatened species can, if regulated properly, actually help save a species. That's one reason why Zimbabwe's proposals have drawn a surprising amount of cautious support.

The secretariat of CITES has come out in support of Zimbabwe's proposals. The World Wildlife Fund, which has historically tended toward the pure protection positions, favors removal of the "endangered species" label from elephants, but wants the ivory trade ban to remain at least for another two years. The United States, while commending Zimbabwe's efforts to protect elephants, opposes lifting the ban. [Editor's note: CITES voted in June 1997 to downgrade the protected status of elephants in Zimbabwe, Namibia, and Botswana, allowing the selling of ivory stockpiles beginning in March 1999.]

One vocal proponent of sustainable utilization is Buck DeVries, the managing director of Gwayi Conservancy, a fenced area within Zimbabwe's Hwange National Park where hunting is allowed. He stands in the middle of his land, sporting mutton-chop sideburns, wearing shoes made from elephant hide. His pet lion sits nearby.

"We want the elephant to be a commodity, because if it isn't, it might as well be dead." DeVries is an ex-rancher, but doesn't regret his career change: "All our cattle were killed by the wildlife from the parks, so I finally figured, if you can't beat them, join them."

DeVries sells hunting licenses now and makes 10 times the money he earned from ranching. The few elephant-hunting licenses granted are issued only to kill elderly bulls, a group DeVries has no patience for. "Big bulls—they don't breed, they just fight. Fifty percent of them die anyway because they kill each other, or they die in the water and no one makes any money. Maybe it's good for the leopards and the hyena, but nature is our living."

SUSTAINABLE UTILIZATION

DeVries's observations are in line with studies commissioned by the World Wildlife Fund. Cattle ranching is a fraction as lucrative as wildlife, and does more harm to the terrain. DeVries does keep some cattle—mostly as food for his crocodile farm.

In fact, crocodiles are the golden example of sustainable utilization. Sixteen years ago, they were almost extinct, until the government here gave landowners permission to collect their eggs and incubate them. In the wild, crocodile eggs have a 2 percent chance of making it to adulthood. In captivity, the crocodiles had a 95 percent survival rate and 1.5 million of them survived that first incubation. Of that number, about 20,000 were set free in national parks, the rest raised for their hides. Today the wild population is stable, if not excessive. "You know why?" DeVries asks, lighting another cigarette. "Money."

In the communal lands around Zimbabwe's national parks, elephants are feared and dreaded. In a single hour, an elephant can destroy an acre of corn—and often does. "They come back year after year," says Christophe Atube, a village official in the Tsholotsho district, arid woodlands that abut Hwange National Park. "Sometimes a herd will split into groups, raid different fields, join up afterward and move away. We can do nothing."

Yet the Tsholotsho district owes much to these animals. Under Zimbabwe's Campfire program, or Communal Areas Management Programme for Indigenous Resources, villages are compensated for damage from elephants and other wildlife through revenue from hunting licenses; a license to kill one bull costs $8,000.

IVORY BAN INEFFECTIVE

TRAFFIC, a global environmental network that tracks unlawful trade in animal parts, had recently concluded in a report sponsored by the World Conservation Union, the Species Survival Commission, the World Wildlife Fund, and the U.S. Fish and Wildlife Service that the CITES ban on ivory trade was not living up to expectations. The ivory trade had not stopped, and the rate of elephant poaching, after a brief fall in the early '90s, was now on the upswing. Moreover, the ban had done nothing to stem the greatest threat to elephants: the loss of habitat worldwide to a growing human population.

Karl Hess Jr., *Reason*, October 1997.

"When people see an elephant, they also see money," says Taurai Dube, the district manager. But according to the Zimbabwean government, Campfire isn't seeing enough money. "We are praying for an electric fence," says Dube, referring to one of the few barriers elephants respect, a project that could be funded by the sale of hunting licenses for another dozen or so elephants—but that will take another few years. Tantalizingly, a more immediate source for funding is sitting only a few hundred miles away in "Fort Knox" in Harare in the form of 30 tons of ivory. A fraction of the money from the sale of this ivory to the Japanese could finance the Campfire program and more electric fences.

If you want to see the unintended consequences of protecting endangered species, take a look at Zimbabwe's baobab trees. These trees, which can live for more than 1,000 years, thrive in semi-desert areas. When Zimbabwe created many of its national parks 20 years ago, the baobabs thrived. But now most of the trees are ringed with deep scars carved by elephants with their tusks while foraging. Many of the trees, after surviving hundreds of years, have fallen over and died. One by Victoria Falls has an armed guard, making sure elephants and tourists stay away.

The fact is, it is not easy to live with elephants. They do not tread lightly. They are impatient, finicky eaters, daily consuming around 50 gallons of water and 250 pounds of grass and leaves. They browse—meaning they strip leaves off branches with their trunks and eat them. They uproot trees to get to tasty seed pods on top, eat for a few minutes and move on. Elephants are partial to maize and sorghum, adore watermelon and, true to cliché, they never forget where they have grazed before. As their population grows, going from around 50,000 in 1989 to more than 60,000 in 1997 (according to government estimates), the impact on the land intensifies.

CULLING ELEPHANTS

So it is expensive for Zimbabwe to manage its elephants. Right now, the country has the legal right to cull its elephant herds to prevent overpopulation. (The CITES agreement affects only trade laws, not internal control.) But the government estimates that it costs about $350 to kill one elephant and killing more than one is usually necessary. Elephants live to about 65 in matriarchal groups, and have strong, eerily humanlike ties to each other. They communicate through infrasound—noises too low for humans to hear—and touch each other constantly with their trunks. Elephants nurse for two years and, if orphaned, are rarely, if ever, adopted by other herds. Herds do not function well without a matriarch, so culling them requires killing an entire family group. Sometimes groups numbering more than 20 must be shot at once. The tusks are then removed and taken to "Fort Knox."

It is a gory sight, one that was used very effectively in direct mailings by the major wildlife organizations advocating pure protection to rally support for the 1989 trade ban. Gunning down a large, intelligent animal that is probably older than the human who fires the shot seems to many people in the United States—a nation with a multibillion dollar pet industry and the home of People for the Ethical Treatment of Animals—the height of barbarity. Somehow, the sight of a toppled 1,000-year-old tree, tusked to death by too many elephants, or a rural farmer complaining about his season's work destroyed by a single elephant, isn't nearly as heart-wrenching.

PENALIZED FOR SUCCESS

But elephants in southern Africa are not endangered and living with these animals is a different story than seeing them in a zoo, on the Discovery Channel or an occasional trip. Zimbabwe is one of the most politically stable African nations, and has (with the exception of the rhino, which has been poached almost to extinction all over the continent) successfully managed its wildlife. The ivory-trade ban effectively penalizes Zimbabwe for supporting a healthy population of elephants.

Elephants are perfectly capable of paying their own way in southern Africa. It's simply a matter of allowing it.

PERIODICAL BIBLIOGRAPHY

The following articles have been selected to supplement the diverse views presented in this chapter. Addresses are provided for periodicals not indexed in the *Readers' Guide to Periodical Literature*, the *Alternative Press Index*, the *Social Sciences Index*, or the *Index to Legal Periodicals and Books*.

ActionLine	"Elephants Must 'Pay Their Way' to Survive," Fall 1997. Available from Friends of Animals, 777 Post Rd., Darien, CT 06820 or http://www.enviroweb.org/foa/global/c1.htm.
Stephanie Boyd	"Egos and Elephants," *New Internationalist*, March 1997.
Stephen Budiansky	"Killing with Kindness," *U.S. News & World Report*, November 25, 1996.
Victoria Butler	"Is This Any Way to Save Africa's Wildlife?" *International Wildlife*, March/April 1995.
Andre Carothers	"Market Solutions," *E Magazine*, January/February 1994.
Jonathan Fisher	"To Ban or Not to Ban," *International Wildlife*, May/June 1997.
Karl Hess Jr.	"Wild Success," *Reason*, October 1997.
Akin L. Mabogunje	"The Environmental Challenges in Sub-Saharan Africa," *Environment*, May 1995.
Donald G. McNeil Jr.	"The Fencing of Africa," *New York Times Magazine*, December 14, 1997.
Robert H. Nelson	"Calvinism Minus God," *Forbes*, October 5, 1998.
Mark Owens and Delia Owens	"Can Time Heal Zambia's Elephants?" *International Wildlife*, May/June 1997.
Allan Richards	"The Elephant War," *Utne Reader*, November/December 1996.
Matthew Scully	"Kill an Elephant, Save an Elephant," *New York Times*, August 2, 1997.
Mwamba H.A. Shete	"Kenya Seeks Home for Nation's Wildlife," *Forum for Applied Research and Public Policy*, Summer 1997.
Chris Styles and David Barritt	"African Elephants Under the Gun," *Animals' Agenda*, September/October 1997.
Teresa M. Telecky	"The Smoke Screen of CAMPFIRE," *Animals' Agenda*, January/February 1997.
Ken Wells	"Animal Farm," *Wall Street Journal*, January 7, 1997.

FOR FURTHER DISCUSSION

CHAPTER 1

1. Chen Chimutengwende and Dennis Brutus argue that history is repeating itself because, in their view, African nations are being recolonized by outside powers. What evidence do they provide to support their assertions? Are their arguments, in your view, convincing? Why or why not?

2. Alassane D. Ouattara, Evangelos A. Calamitsis, and Jack Boorman are all officials of the International Monetary Fund. Should their positions within this organization affect your evaluation of their arguments concerning the IMF, as well as Africa's debt and economic development? Explain.

3. What concerns and objections about foreign aid programs does Isaias Afwerki raise? Are these concerns addressed in the viewpoint by George E. Moose regarding the goals and methods of foreign aid? If so, are they addressed adequately, in your opinion? Why or why not?

4. How does Veronica Brand translate Africa's debt crisis into "human terms"? What makes this an effective argumentative device, in your opinion?

CHAPTER 2

1. Both Amadu Sesay and Ikaweba Bunting discuss the influences of foreign nations on African politics and conflicts. On what points do their analyses of such foreign influence converge? On what points to they diverge? Explain.

2. What point is Ikaweba Bunting attempting to make with his opening anecdote? Does his illustration, in your view, successfully support his arguments about nation building and conflict in Africa? Why or why not?

3. Vincent D. Kern II argues that several safeguards exist to ensure that U.S. military training and equipment provided to African military units are not used wrongfully. Do you believe he has adequately addressed the concerns raised by Scott Nathanson? Explain why or why not.

4. After reading the viewpoints of Alain Destexhe and Leo J. De-Souza, do you believe that the history of past atrocities between the Hutus and Tutsis provides any mitigating factors in judging people accused of genocide in Rwanda? Explain your answer.

Chapter 3

1. Both David F. Gordon and Keith B. Richburg make recommendations on U.S. policy toward Africa that they believe can promote democracy. What are the main differences between their prescriptions? Whose recommendations, in your view, seem more likely to succeed? Explain.

2. What personal qualities of President Nelson Mandela does Anthony Lewis describe? What importance does Lewis attach to them for assessing South Africa's human rights situation? Does a different picture of Mandela emerge from Newton Kanhema's criticisms of South Africa's government? Justify your answers.

Chapter 4

1. Ian Player and Henri Nsanjama both refer to the legacy of Europe's colonization of Africa in relation to the creation of national parks and wilderness areas. Discuss how each author's arguments concerning this colonial legacy strengthen or weaken their contentions on present wildlife conservation polices. Which do you think presents stronger arguments? Explain.

2. What, according to Nsanjama, is the "key" to successful African wildlife conservation? Judging from the viewpoint presented, do you believe Ian Player agrees or disagrees with Nsanjama on this point? Explain your answer.

3. After reading the arguments presented by CAMPFIRE and David Barrit on the pros and cons of wildlife hunting, place yourself in the position of a villager who lives in close vicinity of elephant populations. Would you be more or less likely to support hunting programs such as CAMPFIRE? Should the views of people who live close to elephants carry greater weight than the opinions of city dwellers and people outside of Africa? Why or why not?

4. As revealed in the viewpoints by Wendy Marston and Abdul Shareef, much of the support for relaxing the ivory trade ban comes from southern African nations including Zimbabwe and Botswana, while opposition to this initiative comes from eastern African nations such as Tanzania and Kenya. What does this reveal about ascertaining the "African" position on this issue? What possible solutions to this controversy would you recommend?

CHRONOLOGY OF EVENTS

4000 B.C.– 1500 B.C.	Climate changes transform Saharan region from grassland to desert, creating a barrier inhibiting easy movement of people between northern Africa and the rest of the continent.
3100 B.C.	Upper and Lower Egypt are unified, marking the rise of what is recognized as Africa's first major civilization.
1000 B.C.– A.D. 400	Bantu-speaking people gradually spread from what is now the Nigeria-Cameroon border downward into central and southern Africa, spreading their knowledge of farming and ironworking and displacing indigenous Mbuti (Pygmy) and Khoisan (Bushman) peoples.
100 B.C.	Cities on the eastern Africa coast develop trade with the Middle East and South Asia.
300–500	Christianity spreads through northern Africa and influences the development of Egypt, Aksum (Ethiopia), and the Nile Valley region of Nubia.
600–1600	West Africa witnesses the rise of powerful kingdoms, including Ghana, Mali, and the Songhai Empire, that grow rich on trade between that region and North Africa.
639–710	Arab Muslims conquer Egypt and the rest of northern Africa, spreading Islam to the continent.
1100s	Arab and Persian Muslims settle in the east coast of Africa and develop city-states and trade with India, Indonesia, and countries bordering the Red Sea and Persian Gulf.
1200–1500	Major kingdoms are established in central and southern Africa, including the Kongo, Luba, and the Mwanamutapa Empire (Zimbabwe).
1400s	Portugal begins era of European exploration and conquest of Africa. The Portuguese establish trading posts on Africa's west coast, attempt to convert rulers of the African state of Kongo to Christianity, and ship black Africans back to Europe as slaves.
	Cattle-herding Tutsi people migrate into the area of what is now Rwanda and Burundi and establish monarchial kingdoms over the agricultural Hutu.
1497–1498	Three Portuguese ships under Vasco Da Gama successfully sail around Africa's southern and eastern coasts.
1500s	Portugal seizes control of East Africa's city-states in an effort to monopolize trade.
1518	A Spanish vessel brings the first shipment of slaves brought directly from Africa to the Americas. Over the next 350 years an estimated 20 to 30 million Africans are kidnapped and taken to North and South America as slaves. A smaller established trade on Africa's east coast exports slaves to Middle East and Asian countries. Aided by purchased European firearms, the capture and sale of slaves becomes a primary industry for many African societies.

1652	The Dutch East India Company builds a depot for provisions at the southern tip of Africa. Cape Province becomes the first *Boer* (Dutch for farmer) colony in South Africa. Dutch and French colonists begin to spread in surrounding regions.
1700s	Arabs from Oman expel the Portuguese from the East African coast; they dominate the African coast until the nineteenth century.
1770s	Two groups migrating in search of land meet in southern Africa: Dutch settlers, moving eastward from Cape Town, encounter Bantu-speaking peoples migrating south and west.
1800s	Europeans extend exploration of Africa's interior.
1814	Great Britain gains Cape Province from the Dutch by purchase; significant numbers of British colonists arrive in the 1820s.
1818–1828	The Zulu warrior Shaka begins a campaign of military conquest that makes the Zulus a powerful empire and sets in force the *mfecane*—a period of forced migrations of conquered and uprooted peoples in southern Africa.
1821	Monrovia is founded on Africa's northwest coast by the American Colonization Society as a haven for freed American slaves. The first group of settlers arrives in 1822.
1835–1843	In what became known as the *Great Trek*, Dutch settlers of Cape Colony migrate from Cape Province to the interior of southern Africa to escape British rule. These Afrikaners defeat Zulu forces in the 1838 Battle of Blood River, and establish independent republics of Transvaal in 1852 and Orange Free State in 1854.
1838	Monrovia joins with neighboring settlements of former American and European slaves to form the commonwealth of Liberia. It becomes an independent republic in 1847.
1854	South Africa is divided into four provinces with the two coastal provinces going to the British and the inland provinces to the Dutch.
1880–1912	All parts of Africa except Liberia and Ethiopia become colonies or protectorates of European nations. Colonial rule is established peacefully in some instances, while in other cases is met with violent resistance.
1884	The Berlin Conference establishes boundaries for European claims on African territory.
1894	Germany colonizes the kingdoms of Ruanda and Urundi (Rwanda and Burundi) as part of German East Africa; Tutsi elite are maintained in positions of power.
1899–1902	The British defeat the Boers in the Boer War; South Africa is brought within the British Commonwealth.
1908	King Leopold II of Belgium is forced to relinquish his personal rule of the Congo to Belgium. A public commission of inquiry found that Africans under his rule were victims of a slave-labor system and other abuses.

The British and Afrikaners form the Union of South Africa; Africans, Coloreds, and Asians are excluded from government.

1912   In South Africa, the African National Congress is formed to defend the political rights of blacks.

1920s   European colonial rule of Africa is firmly established. Germany's possessions are redistributed among the Allies after World War I.

1922   Egypt attains a limited measure of sovereign independence.

1930   Revelations of connivance with forced labor practices tantamount to slavery cause the government of Liberia to fall. Reforms end the labor practices, but Americo-Liberians (descendants of resettled American slaves) still dominate the country and indigenous African people are still treated as second-class citizens with few rights.

1939–1945   African colonies side mostly with the Allies in World War II; fighting occurs primarily in North Africa. European colonial powers are weakened by the war, while the international position of the United States and Soviet Union is strengthened.

1947   Jomo Kenyatta becomes president of the Kenya African Union, a political party formed in 1944 to organize opposition to British colonial rule.

1948   South Africa institutes a policy of rigid racial separation (*apartheid*).

1952–1954   Egyptian military officers overthrow the monarchy and negotiate the withdrawal of British forces.

1952-1956   Fighting between Kenyan nationalists (called Mau Maus) and British colonial forces results in the killing of 13,000 Africans, 95 Europeans, and 129 Asians, according to official figures. Nationalist leader Jomo Kenyatta is imprisoned from 1953 to 1961.

1954–1962   Algerian nationalists fight a guerrilla war against the French. Thirteen thousand French troops and 145,000 Algerians are killed before Algeria wins independence.

1957   Ghana becomes the first sub-Saharan African country to gain independence from its colonial rulers; Kwame Nkrumah, a rebel leader since 1947, leads its new government. Other countries gain independence over the next decade.

1959   Clashes of ethnic violence in Rwanda erupt between its Tutsi and Hutu peoples; thousands of Tutsi refugees flee the nation, which becomes formally independent of Belgian rule in 1962.

1960   South Africa outlaws the African National Congress (ANC).

Nigeria becomes independent from Great Britain; ethnic groups compete for political power.

Belgium grants the Belgian Congo independence; the nation, renamed Congo, is soon engulfed in civil disorder. United Nations troops are sent at the invitation of the country's government to restore order; they remain until 1963.

1961	A guerrilla war in Angola is launched by rebels against Portugal, which refuses to relinquish its African colonial possessions.
1963	Nelson Mandela and other African National Congress (ANC) leaders are imprisoned in South Africa under its Suppression of Communism Act.
	The Organization of African Unity is founded.
	Sylvanus Olympio of Togo is assassinated by a group of dissatisfied ex-soldiers; it is the first of more than seventy military coups in thirty-two African nations between 1962 and 1997.
	Refugee Tutsi invade Rwanda and are defeated; thousands of Tutsi flee Rwanda to Burundi, Uganda, Congo, and Tanzania.
1964	The Front for the Liberation of Mozambique (FRELIMO) launches a revolt against Portuguese rule.
1965	White settlers declare Rhodesia independent and form a white-dominated government; Great Britain enacts economic sanctions.
	Joseph Mobutu stages a coup leaving him in power in the Congo; he later changes the country's name to Zaire and his own name to Mobutu Sese Seko.
1966	Nigeria suffers the first of five military coups over the next twenty years.
1967	Kenya, Tanzania, and Uganda form the East African Community to promote trade and to cooperate in administering railways and airports; the organization ceases operations in 1977.
1967–1970	Civil war erupts in Nigeria after its eastern region attempts to establish the independent republic of Biafra; it ends when Biafra surrenders.
1971	Idi Amin takes over the government of Uganda.
1972	The Tutsi-dominated government of Burundi survives an attempted Hutu rebellion; at least 100,000 Hutu are killed in retaliation and 150,000 Hutu flee to neighboring countries including Rwanda.
1973	Juvénal Habyarimana, a Hutu general, leads a coup and becomes head of government in Rwanda.
1974	Emperor Haile Selassie of Ethiopia, who has reigned since 1929, is deposed by the Ethiopian military.
1975	Portugal becomes the last European country with large African holdings to give up its colonies. In Mozambique, power is handed to the FRELIMO, who attempts to establish a Marxist state. In Angola, three competing rebel groups vie for control of the country.
1975–1992	The National Mozambican Resistance (RENAMO) engages in a war of terror against Mozambique's peasants and government. RENAMO is supported by the white-minority governments of Rhodesia and South Africa. Peace accords ending the war are signed in October 1992. Multiparty elections are held in October 1992.

1976	The Popular Movement for the Liberation of Angola (MPLA), assisted by Soviet arms and Cuban troops, gains the upper hand after months of fighting over its rivals and is recognized as the legitimate government of Angola. The National Front for the Liberation of Angola (FNLA) collapses, formally surrendering to the government in 1984. However, Jonas Savimbi, leader of the Union for the Total Independence of Angola (UNITA), retreats to southern Angola and continues a guerrilla warfare campaign with assistance from South Africa and the United States.
1977	The leftist government of Ethiopia, led by chief of staff and self-proclaimed Marxist Mengistu Haile Mariam, expels U.S. troops and courts the Soviet Union.
	In South Africa, black political activist Steven Biko is killed while in police custody.
1978	Kenyan president Jomo Kenyatta dies; vice president Daniel arap Moi succeeds him.
1979	An army of Tanzanians and exiled Ugandans occupy the Ugandan capital city, Kampala, and force dictator Idi Amin out of the country.
	Black Africans in Rhodesia gain control of the government and end white-minority rule; country is renamed Zimbabwe in 1980.
1980	Army sergeant Samuel K. Doe leads a military coup that overthrows the government of Liberia, ends over a century of Americo-Liberian domination of the country, and suspends the country's 1847 constitution.
1980s	Drought and warfare bring serious famine to parts of Africa, including Ethiopia.
1985	The South African government declares a state of emergency in the face of rising resistance; the United States and eleven European nations impose economic sanctions on South Africa.
	Samuel K. Doe wins presidential elections in Liberia.
1986	Yoweri Museveni leads a successful military takeover of the government of Uganda. His regime stresses national unity and economic growth. Museveni, who wins presidential elections held in 1996, becomes a leading figure among the so-called "new generation" of African leaders.
1988	Angola, South Africa, and Cuba sign a peace agreement calling for the independence of Namibia and an end to South African and Cuban military involvement in Angola.
	South African president P.W. Botha renews state of emergency for another year. Government increases media restrictions.
1989	Frederik W. de Klerk replaces P.W. Botha as president of South Africa.
1990	The collapse of the Soviet Union and the end of the cold war between the Soviet Union and the United States marks an end to the era in which the two superpowers competed for allies and client states on the African continent.

President Samuel K. Doe of Liberia is killed as the country enters a state of civil war. A multinational West African peacekeeping force, led by Nigeria, is sent to maintain order, but fails to halt the fighting between government forces and multiple rebel armies.

Namibia gains independence after seventy-five years of control by South Africa.

South African president de Klerk legalizes the African National Congress and other opposition groups; Nelson Mandela is released from prison. The ANC formally renounces the use of violence and engages in talks with the government.

Rwandese exiles in Uganda launch a rebellion; Belgium and several African nations send troops to Rwanda to support the government.

1991   In Ethiopia, the government of Mengistu Haile Mariam falls to rebels who promise a transition to multiparty government.

The South African parliament repeals the Population Registration Act of 1948 and other apartheid legislation; President George Bush lifts U.S. sanctions against South Africa.

Following political unrest, Kenya's constitution is amended to allow for multiple political parties.

Muhammad Siad Barre, military ruler of Somalia since 1969, flees the country as it descends into anarchy and conflict. Over the next 23 months an estimated 50,000 Somalians are killed in factional fighting and 300,000 starve to death due to war-related food shortages.

A peace accord is negotiated between the MPLA government and UNITA rebels in Angola, calling for elections in 1992.

1992   UNITA leader Jonas Savimbi loses multiparty elections in Angola. He refuses to accept the results and resumes war against the government.

Despite increasing charges of corruption and human rights violations, Kenyan president Daniel arap Moi is reelected in Kenya's first multiparty elections in twenty-six years.

U.S. Marines intervene in Somalia to assist the United Nations in restoring order and distributing food.

1993   Negotiators representing the South African government and the African National Congress (ANC) and other political organizations reach an agreement on an interim constitution for South Africa and elections open to all races in 1994.

Eritrea secedes from Ethiopia and becomes an independent nation.

A Tutsi coup in Burundi results in the death of Melchior Mdadaye, a Hutu who had won the country's first multiparty presidential election; the ensuing violence results in 100,000 deaths and 700,000 refugees.

1994	Rwanda's president Habyarimana is killed in a plane crash. Rwanda's government and military launch a campaign to exterminate Tutsis in Rwanda. The Tutsi-led Rwandan Patriotic Front seizes control of the country, causing more refugees to flee.

1994   Rwanda's president Habyarimana is killed in a plane crash. Rwanda's government and military launch a campaign to exterminate Tutsis in Rwanda. The Tutsi-led Rwandan Patriotic Front seizes control of the country, causing more refugees to flee.

South Africa holds multiracial elections; the ANC wins 62.9 percent of the vote; Nelson Mandela is elected president.

The government of Angola and UNITA sign new peace accords to end the country's twenty-year civil war. United Nations peacekeeping forces are sent to oversee demobilization of troops.

Nigeria's military government under Sani Abacha arrests Moshood Abiola for treason after Abiola declares himself the legitimate winner of Nigeria's 1993 presidential elections.

U.S. troops withdraw from Somalia after suffering 30 casualties and 175 wounded.

1995   A United Nations war crimes tribunal is established in Tanzania to try suspected perpetrators of genocide in Rwanda.

Of the world's estimated 18.4 million people living with AIDS, sixty percent are in sub-Saharan Africa.

The military government of Nigeria, despite international outcry, hangs writer and dissident Ken Saro-Wiwa and eight others. Saro-Wiwa had protested the government's treatment of his Ogoni tribe and the environmental damage caused by oil drilling in his homeland.

1996   Nigeria helps broker a peace agreement ending civil war in Liberia; over the previous seven years 150,000 Liberians had been killed and more than half of its 2.8 million population left homeless.

Forty-nine African countries sign the Treaty of Pelindaba to make the continent a nuclear-weapon-free zone.

1.5 million Hutu refugees return to Rwanda from Zaire (Congo) and Tanzania.

1997   Laurent Kabila proclaims himself president of Zaire, renaming it the Democratic Republic of Congo. Longtime dictator Mobutu Sese Seko flees the country and later dies in exile.

Rebel leader Charles Taylor wins presidential elections in Liberia.

1998   U.S. President Bill Clinton makes an eleven-day trip to Africa in March, visiting six countries.

Many African nations are involved in Congo's civil war. Zimbabwe, Angola, and Namibia send troops in support of the government of Laurent Kabila. Ethnic Tutsis in Zaire, aided by the governments of Uganda and Rwanda (former allies of Kabila), comprise a large portion of the rebel forces.

Nigeria intervenes in Sierra Leone to restore the country's first democratically elected president, Ahmed Tejan Kabbah, after a military coup had forced him out of office.

Border dispute between Eritrea and Ethiopia threatens to erupt to war.

A United Nations report accuses Rwanda's government and forces loyal to Congo president Laurent Kabila of atrocities against Rwandan Hutu refugees.

After more than two years of hearings, South Africa's Truth and Reconciliation Commission releases its report on apartheid-era atrocities.

The deaths of military dictator Sani Abacha and prominent dissident Moshood Abiola widen political fissures in Nigeria. New leader Abdulsalam Abubakar frees political prisoners and promises elections and a return to civilian rule in 1999.

Organizations to Contact

The editors have compiled the following list of organizations concerned with the issues debated in this book. The descriptions are derived from materials provided by the organizations. All have publications or information available for interested readers. The list was compiled on the date of publication of the present volume; the information provided here may change. Be aware that many organizations take several weeks or longer to respond to inquiries, so allow as much time as possible.

Africa Faith and Justice Network (AFJN)
PO Box 29378, Washington, DC 20017
(202) 832-3412
e-mail: afjn@afjn.org • website: http://www.acad.cua.edu/afjn

The network comprises religious groups concerned with oppression and injustice in Africa. It analyzes how U.S. foreign policy affects Africa and challenges policies it believes are detrimental to Africans. The network publishes the bimonthly *Around Africa* newsletter, *Action Alerts*, and quarterly documentation pamphlets.

Africa News Service
PO Box 3851, Durham, NC 27702
(919) 286-0747 • fax: (919) 286-2614
e-mail: newsdesk@africanews.org
website: http://www.africanews.org

Africa News Online provides stories from major African news organizations plus key resources on business, politics, science, arts, entertainment, and U.S.–Africa relations. Africa News Service, an award-winning nonprofit agency that has been a leading source of Africa reporting in the United States for two decades, produces the site.

Africa Policy Information Center (APIC)
110 Maryland Ave. NE, Suite 509, Washington, DC 20002
(202) 546-7961 • fax: (202) 546-1545
e-mail: apic@igc.apc.org • website: http://www.africapolicy.org

APIC's primary objective is to widen policy debate about African issues and the U.S. role in Africa. The center concentrates on providing accessible policy-relevant information and analysis that is usable by a wide range of groups and individuals. In particular, APIC identifies critical policy issues in U.S.–African relations; brings diverse perspectives from African and U.S. grassroots groups, scholars, and governmental and nongovernmental participants into the policy process; and makes information and analysis accessible to a broad range of U.S. public constituencies. The center publishes several background papers with titles such as "Africa on the Internet" and "Thinking Regionally: Priorities for U.S. Policy Toward Africa."

Africare

440 R St. NW, Washington, DC 20001

(202) 462-3614 • fax: (202) 387-1034

e-mail: africare@africare.org • website: http://www.africare.org

Africare works to assist the villagers of sub-Saharan Africa to develop water, agricultural, health, and environmental resources. The organization has offices in twenty-eight African nations to assist in the development of rural Africa. It publishes an annual report as well as pamphlets such as *Food in Africa*, *African Development: The Big Picture*, and *Homeless in Africa*.

Black Eagle Publishing

14 College Rd., Rondebosch, 7700, South Africa

e-mail: wildmags@iafrica.com

website: http://www.discover-africa.com

Black Eagle Publishing is a small independent publishing company based in Cape Town, South Africa. Currently the company produces three magazines, *Africa—Environment & Wildlife*, *Africa—Birds & Birding*, and *Discover Africa*. Its website offers all three, along with extensive information on every country in Africa.

Institute for Food and Development Policy/Food First

398 60th St., Oakland, CA 94618

(510) 654-4400 • fax: (510) 654-4551

e-mail: foodfirst@foodfirst.org • website: http://www.foodfirst.org

The institute is a member-supported nonprofit research and education center committed to developing solutions to hunger and poverty around the world and establishing food as a fundamental human right. Its publications include *World Hunger: Twelve Myths* as well as numerous articles, reports, and policy briefs.

MBendi Information Services

PO Box 23498, Claremont, 7735, South Africa

+27 (0)21-616-316 • fax: +27 (0)21-616-316

e-mail: MBendi@mbendi.co.za • website: http://www.mbendi.co.za

Founded in 1995, MBendi Information Services is an African company that provides consulting services in the areas of Africa and the African oil industry. It is also the creator of the AfroPaedia website, which is accessible from its homepage, and is considered Africa's premier business site. AfroPaedia assists companies and businesspeople around the world doing business in and with Africa.

Peace Parks Foundation

Groot Paardevlei, 29 Magnolia St., Somerset West, 7129, South Africa

+27 21 855-3564 • fax: +27 21 855-3958

e-mail: parks@ppf.org.za • website: http://www.peaceparks.org.za

The Peace Parks Foundation's primary objective is to promote transfrontier conservation areas—"peace parks"—in Africa. Its members work toward this goal through fund-raising, working with conservation and community organizations, and developing the ecotourism industry in Africa. The foundation publishes an annual report as well as the *Peace Parks Newsletter*.

Population Institute
107 Second St. NE, Washington, DC 20002
(202) 544-3300 • fax: (202) 544-0068
e-mail: web@populationinstitute.org
website: http://www.populationinstitute.org

The Population Institute is dedicated to decreasing the rate of population growth in the Third World. It encourages leaders and the media to draw the public's attention to the problems of overpopulation. To promote its cause, the institute publishes the bimonthly newsletter *Popline* and the report *1997 World Population Overview*.

U.S.–Africa Free Enterprise Education Foundation and Business Association
400 N. Tampa St., Suite 1120, Tampa, FL 33602
(813) 301-8723 • fax: (813) 301-9301
website: http://www.usafrica.com

The foundation promotes both free enterprise and humanitarianism. It organizes economic, educational, and cultural programs and events that transcend racial, ethnic, and religious divisions in the United States and Africa. It offers several Africa-related magazines and publications on its website, a kid's corner with quizzes on Africa, and a weather update on all African countries.

U.S. State Department Bureau of African Affairs
U.S. Department of State
2201 C St. NW, Washington, DC 20520
(202) 647-4000
e-mail: secretary@state.gov
website: http://www.state.gov/www/regions/africa

The bureau is responsible for advising the secretary of state and guiding the operation of U.S. diplomatic establishment in the countries of sub-Saharan Africa. It offers fact sheets and background information on Africa as well as up-to-date news briefings and press statements on U.S.–African policy.

WildNet Africa
Box 73528, Lynnwood Ridge, 0400, South Africa
+27-12-991-3083 • fax: +27-12-991-3851
e-mail: basecamp@wildnetafrica.com
website: http://www.wildnetafrica.com

WildNet Africa creates and maintains websites for a variety of wildlife- and travel-related enterprises in Africa. Its website contains the latest news on African wildlife conservation efforts, antipoaching patrols, and facts on African wildlife.

BIBLIOGRAPHY OF BOOKS

Jonathan S. Adams and
Thomas O. McShane
The Myth of Wild Africa: Conservation Without Illusion.
Reprint ed. Berkeley and Los Angeles: University
of California Press, 1996.

Howard Adelman and
Astri Suhrke, eds.
*The Path of a Genocide: The Rwanda Crisis from Uganda to
Zaire.* Somerset, NJ: Transaction, 1998.

Claude Ake
Democracy and Development in Africa. Washington, DC:
Brookings Institution, 1996.

George Akeya Agbango,
ed.
Issues and Trends in Contemporary African Politics. New
York: Peter Lang, 1997.

Sola Akinrinade and
Amadu Sesay, eds.
Africa in the Post–Cold War International System.
Herndon, VA: Pinter, 1998.

Michael Barratt Brown
Africa's Choices. Boulder, CO: Westview, 1995.

L. Dalton Casto
*The Dilemmas of Africanization: Choices and Dangers for
Sub-Saharan Africa.* Moraga, CA: African Ways, 1998.

James Ciment
*Angola and Mozambique: Postcolonial Wars in Southern
Africa.* New York: Facts On File, 1997.

Carol Cunningham
Horn of Darkness: Rhinos on the Edge. New York: Oxford
University Press, 1997.

Francis M. Deng
et al., eds.
Sovereignty as Responsibility: Conflict Management in Africa.
Washington, DC: Brookings Institution, 1996.

Alain Destexhe
Rwanda and Genocide in the Twentieth Century. New York:
New York University Press, 1995.

John P. Entelis, ed.
Islam, Democracy, and the State in North Africa. Bloom-
ington: Indiana University Press, 1997.

Robert Garfield
The Concise History of Africa. Acton, MA: Copley,
1994.

Philip Gourevitch
*We Wish to Inform You That Tomorrow We Will Be Killed
with Our Families: Stories from Rwanda.* New York:
Farrar, Straus and Giroux, 1998.

Hélène Grandvoinnet
and Hartmut Schneider,
eds.
Conflict Management in Africa: A Permanent Challenge.
Paris: Development Centre of the Organisation
for Economic Co-operation and Development,
1998.

Margaret Jean Hay
and Sharon Stichter, eds.
African Women South of the Sahara. 2nd ed. New York:
John Wiley & Sons, 1995.

Kempe Ronald Hope,
ed.
*Structural Adjustment, Reconstruction, and Development in
Africa.* Brookfield, VT: Ashgate, 1997.

Nikoi Kote-Nikoi
*Beyond the New Orthodoxy: Africa's Debt and Development
Crisis in Retrospect.* Brookfield, VT: Ashgate, 1996.

Tukumbi Lumumba-Kasongo	*The Rise of Multipartyism and Democracy in the Context of Global Change: The Case of Africa.* Westport, CT: Praeger, 1998.
Michael Maren	*The Road to Hell: The Ravaging Effects of Foreign Aid and International Charity.* New York: Free Press, 1997.
Timothy McKee, ed.	*No More Strangers Now: Young Voices from a New South Africa.* New York: DK, 1998.
Marina Ottaway, ed.	*Democracy in Africa: The Hard Road Ahead.* Boulder, CO: Lynne Rienner, 1997.
John Prendergast	*Frontline Diplomacy: Humanitarian Aid and Conflict in Africa.* Boulder, CO: Lynne Rienner, 1996.
John Reader	*Africa: A Biography of the Continent.* New York: Alfred A. Knopf, 1998.
Keith B. Richburg	*Out of America: A Black Man Confronts Africa.* New York: BasicBooks, 1997.
Randall Robinson	*Defending the Spirit: A Black Life in America.* New York: Dutton, 1998.
Emory Roe	*Except Africa: Remaking Development, Rethinking Power.* Somerset, NJ: Transaction, 1998.
Rukhsana A. Siddiqui, ed.	*Subsaharan Africa in the 1990s: Challenges to Democracy and Development.* Westport, CT: Praeger, 1997.
Gunnar M. Sorbo and Peter Vale, eds.	*Out of Conflict: From War to Peace in Africa.* Uppsala, Sweden: Nordiska Afrikainstitutet, 1997.
F.H. Toase and Edmund James Yorke, eds.	*The New South Africa: Prospects for Domestic and International Security.* New York: St. Martin's, 1998.
E. Ike Udogu, ed.	*Democracy and Democratization in Africa.* New York: E.J. Brill, 1997.
Marq de Villiers and Sheila Hirtle	*Into Africa: A Journey Through the Ancient Empires.* Toronto: Key Porter Books, 1997.
Richard Werbner and Terence Ranger, eds.	*Postcolonial Identities in Africa.* Atlantic Highlands, NJ: Zed Books, 1996.
David Western	*In the Dust of Kilimanjaro.* Washington, DC: Island Press, 1997.
John A. Wiseman, ed.	*Democracy and Political Change in Sub-Saharan Africa.* New York: Routledge, 1995.
Aguibou Y. Yansané, ed.	*Prospects for Recovery and Sustainable Development in Africa.* Westport, CT: Greenwood, 1996.

INDEX